Language, Culture and Young Children:
Developing English in the Multi-Ethnic Nursery and Infant School

Edited by

Pat Pinsent

Principal Lecturer in English
Roehampton Institute

David Fulton Publishers
London

Published in association with the Roehampton Institute

David Fulton Publishers Ltd
2 Barbon Close, London WC1N 3JX

First published in Great Britain by
David Fulton Publishers 1992

British Library Cataloguing in Publication Data

A catalogue record for this book is available from the British Library

ISBN 1-85346-184-9

Typeset by Chapterhouse, Formby, L37 3PX
Printed in Great Britain by BPCC Wheatons Ltd. Exeter

Contents

Notes on Contributors

JOAN ANIM-ADDO is a lecturer in the English Division of the School of Primary Education at Thames Polytechnic.

TONY AYLWIN is Head of English, School of Primary Education, at Thames Polytechnic. He has a particular interest in storytelling in the classroom.

MAURA BLACKBURN is a senior teacher in Southall, with much experience of multi-ethnic classes.

FRAN DUNCAN is Teacher with responsibility for Traveller Education at the Cleveland Centre for Multicultural Education.

JUDITH LAWTON is a Deputy Head of Hounslow Language Service; Primary Team.

PETA LLOYD was formerly Advisory Teacher in English in the London Borough of Ealing and is now Senior Lecturer in Education, Early Years of Schooling, at Westminster College, Oxford.

ROSEMARY MORGAN is a primary teacher and has also worked as schools liaison tutor at Thames Polytechnic. She is course co-ordinator for curriculum on the Roehampton Institute B.Ed. (In-Service) degree.

PAT PINSENT has worked for many years at Roehampton on various INSET courses in Language and Reading, including the MA (Educational Studies). She teaches English, including Children's Literature, to undergraduates.

DAVID REID is a senior lecturer in Education at the Roehampton Institute, and has worked extensively in the area of racial equality.

CHRISTINE STEVENSON is a senior lecturer in Education at St. Mary's College, Strawberry Hill.

LINDA THOMAS is a senior lecturer in English Language at the Roehampton Institute.

SHÂN WAREING is a lecturer in English language at the Roehampton Institute.

Introduction

If there is one philosophy which unites all the contributors to this book it is the belief that the many varieties of language, dialect, culture and ethnic origin to be found in contemporary Britain should be seen as assets rather than as problems. Certainly, they can sometimes cause difficulties for teachers and administrators, not to mention the children and their parents, but the result of facing these challenges can be enrichment. As the Bullock Report (1975) said, in a chapter (20) which was encouragingly positive (in spite of being in the Section of the Report on Reading and Language Difficulties!):

> In a linguistically conscious nation in the modern world, we should see it [bilingualism] as an asset . . . (p. 294)

Certainly the past history of Britain reveals how much the English language and culture have been enriched from many sources: invasions of these islands; exploration and colonisation overseas; economic forces such as trade and increasing prosperity, often fostering what was fashionable; influences from other English speaking parts of the world. These are only a few of the forces causing large scale changes over the last thousand years. On a smaller scale, perhaps, have been the effects on our national language and culture of the arrival in this country of groups of people with a diversity of languages, dialects and customs. As David Reid (Chapter One) emphasises, the English language is not an untouched, original heritage which we need to keep sacred in order to bestow it on grateful recipients; we have no monolithic culture which they must assimilate in order to be 'true Britons'!

This book focuses on the language and literacy development of children from a variety of ethnic, cultural and language backgrounds, from the earliest stages up to and including National Curriculum Key Stage One. It starts from the assumption that the children's backgrounds are assets to them and to the Nursery and Infant schools which they attend. In order for children to grow up placing a proper value on themselves and developing a healthy self-image, it is vital that they are aware of the riches of all the cultures which they inherit, at home and at school and probably from other sources too, notably places of worship. It is equally important that teachers have a respect for the languages and cultures of the children, and become conscious of the dangers of eurocentrism in their own attitudes and values.

The issues which are discussed here necessarily include that of racial differences. These are not in themselves problematic; the question of attitudes towards people of different ethnic origins can still, however, be a cause of difficulties in schools and in society at large, in spite of legislation in this area.

Probably the most controversial section of the Cox Report (1989) on *English 5–16* was that dealing with Standard English. The responses of the press and of many politicians showed how little the origin of different varieties of English is understood. This can be a key issue for children whose dialect is undervalued. Linda Thomas and Shân Wareing (Chapter Two) put the status of Standard English into a historical and linguistic perspective, making clear the care the teacher needs to take to avoid confusion in the minds of the majority of children who do not have Standard English as their home variety.

Many children, however, arrive at nursery or infant school without even a minimal knowledge of English since another language has been used in their homes. Questions such as how they should be introduced to English and how much importance should be attached to their own mother tongue in the early years are complex; research findings seem to be somewhat inconclusive (see Swann, 1985, p. 403), partly because a good deal of research into the effects of bilingualism on learning has in the past taken place in totally different settings like Wales and Canada. A detailed study of the performance of South Asian pupils in England (Taylor with Hegarty, 1985) cites a number of results, the general applicability of which, however, is affected by the variety of different conditions which exist even in different parts of England. It is, however, clear that much depends on how society in general and the school in particular value the children's first language. The attitude and command of English of their parents are also key factors.

There is some evidence (Downing, 1979, p. 39) that children may learn more easily to read in English if they are initially presented with books in their mother tongue, so that they are not involved in two very demanding kinds of learning at the same time: the reading process and second language acquisition. Unless, however, the school is particularly fortunate in having staff available from a large range of language backgrounds, many children will not have the chance of hearing, let alone reading, their first language in school. Bilingual texts, if they are equal in quality to monolingual ones in their print, illustrations and accuracy, can perhaps go some way towards alleviating this potential difficulty.

Parents may not always, however, want their children's home language to be used in school, even where this is possible. An example is cited by Walsh (in (ed.) Straker-Welds, 1984, p. 24) of a French man who insisted that no French should be spoken to his daughter. Her progress in English was slight until her Nursery school teacher greeted her in French and thus, implicitly, gave recognition to her home language. After this her progress was rapid.

In the past, a good deal of language teaching was carried out in groups temporarily withdrawn from the classroom. Today it is more common to have support teachers in the classroom, who, together with the class teacher, facilitate the process of acquisition of English with well chosen material and judicious use of peer support. Fortunately, children of the age with which we are concerned here have better abilities in acquiring language than older children. It is clear, however, that for children of any age to learn most effectively, language needs to be encountered in a context which has meaning, such as an activity or a story. Adults may have to beware of a natural tendency to want to explain language rules or to 'translate' individual words for children. An example may make this clearer: an English child of nearly three, on holiday in France, was capable of using 'Merci' in contexts where she would use 'Thank you' at home, but completely incapable of understanding the concept of translation: 'What's the French for "Thank you"?'

Whatever our attitude towards the extent to which children should use and develop their own mother tongue, either in school or in supplementary classes arranged by their ethnic community, we need to beware of subconscious assumptions about the superiority of our language and culture to theirs. Even enlightened educators of the recent past can sound a little patronising here. Brown (1979) concludes an eminently practical and sympathetic book (which might, however, today be thought to go too far towards advocating withdrawal of second language children from mainstream classes) with these words:

As teachers in multicultural schools our work is to educate the children in our care, but not transform them. We must have the courage of our convictions to open up avenues leading into the English language and culture, so that the children of other traditions may enter and move forward in our society, but we must never lose the integrity which enables us to recognise and respect those individual qualities which should remain untouched and unchanged – the rightful heritage of each nationality. (p. 167)

The sentiments are in many respects admirable but somewhat one-sided; there seems to be little consciousness of what our society may gain from these other traditions. While these children do need to become competent English speakers in order to have their equal part in our society, we need to acknowledge 'the linguistic resources they bring to learning English' (Meek, 1991, p. 59).

The young child's environment, both linguistic and cultural, will inevitably have had a considerable effect on their cognitive development, even by the time that they arrive in a nursery school or play group. In Chapter Three, Christine Stevenson, with the assistance of Margaret Revell, the Headteacher of a Nursery School, not only elucidates the processes involved but also offers some practical help to the monolingual teacher faced with children whose languages are unknown to her. Rosemary Morgan (Chapter Four) takes the process further, into the Infant School, where the importance of oral language is generally recognised but teachers may sometimes find it difficult to put their priorities into practice in the classroom.

A particular challenge for the teacher occurs when she is faced with children from a culture whose values may seem alien or even radically opposed to her own. This is especially likely in the case of Traveller children; Fran Duncan (Chapter Five) provides some useful information on their background and culture, in order to make it easier for the teacher to empathise with the children as well as to provide material relevant to their literacy development.

Assessment of the language abilities of young children is often difficult for the teacher, even when their first language is English. For bilingual children, the problem is inevitably greater, and there is considerable danger that their abilities will not be recognised and they will be regarded as low achievers. In Chapter Six, Judith Lawton presents some practical suggestions as to how this may be avoided and a realistic assessment made.

A great deal of recent work, on both reading and oral language, stresses the importance of story – so much so that the central section of this book is devoted to this subject, although a consciousness of its centrality also pervades many of the contributions in other sections. Tony Aylwin (Chapter Seven) gives particular attention to the use of traditional stories and shows some of the many values they have in the primary school classroom, as well as indicating some useful sources of such stories.

The debate about the most effective kind of reading material – reading schemes or 'real books' – is generally carried on with little attention to the fact that it is possible that facilitating the acquisition of literacy for children with different social or linguistic backgrounds may well be most effectively done with different kinds of material from that appropriate to first language speakers. In Chapter Eight, Maura Blackburn presents some of the results of her own research project into this question, and offers some practical suggestions for teachers, whatever position they, and the schools in which they teach, take upon this issue.

The selection of books for children making a start on reading should never ignore the way in which books can influence attitudes. In Chapter Nine the attempt is made to assist teachers in forming their own criteria for choosing books within our multicultural society. The need for attention to this matter is certainly not confined to areas where there is a high proportion of children from ethnic minority groups!

Learning to read, listening to stories, being involved in oral language in the classroom, all demand active participation from children. But the writing process is one where the products of the activity of the child become particularly evident to teachers, parents, and other pupils. Peta Lloyd (Chapter Ten) bases her 'question and answer' discussion of children's developmental writing on work done by Chris Norris in her multi-cultural reception class.

Joan Anim-Addo (Chapter Eleven) shows how valuable drama in the classroom can be to the teacher of young children. She provides an answer to the key question, 'How can drama happen in the classroom?' and gives particular attention to how teachers can use the added richness provided by the multi-ethnic dimension.

The concluding section provides a selection of books, addresses of relevant organisations and journals, and non-book resources, which present a positive attitude towards differences in race, language and culture. A short section of pointers toward judgement about the quality of such resources is intended to supplement, rather than replace, the criteria which teachers will want to work out for themselves. They will also no doubt be hoping that their pupils, young as they are, are already implicitly forming positive attitudes towards people of all ethnic groups, cultures and religions, and that all of them will be placing a value upon themselves, their individuality and uniqueness. In perhaps the most frequently quoted words of the Bullock Report (1975):

> No child should be expected to cast off the language and culture of the home as he [or she] crosses the school threshold, nor to live and act as though school and home represent two totally separate and different cultures which have to be kept firmly apart. (p. 287)

PART ONE:

Differences: Problem or Opportunity?

CHAPTER 1

Linguistic Diversity and Equality

David Reid

The challenge

There are few nursery and infant classes in most of the major cities of Great Britain which do not to some extent reflect the linguistic diversity of contemporary Britain. Even in small towns and villages, in parts of the country often described as 'all white', languages other than English are quite often represented in the classroom. Most places, for instance, will have an Indian or Chinese restaurant. The proprietors of these invariably speak a language other than English, in addition to English itself.

Adults whose background is not English will usually either bring up their children, or at the least talk to them, in their 'mother tongue'. Such children will attend the local school for the statutory years. They may well also be found in nursery or other pre-school provision. There are, however, reasons why, in practice, they are less likely to be found in non-statutory provision, especially when they are from the sole family of South or East Asian background in the locality. There is evidence that pre-school provision effectively discriminates against children from minority ethnic groups. This may take the form of staff merely being unwelcoming without intending it, or of using the excuse of not knowing the minority group language concerned. In so far as this kind of practice operates, it amounts to a form of institutionalised racism. Secondly, various traditions and cultural factors concerning child rearing may result in the parents wishing to keep the child at home until official school age. Often these two factors work together with a resultant under-representation of minority ethnic groups and community languages in the under-fives sector.

Linguistic diversity in the classroom is, of course, an asset. Children who speak languages other than English bring variety and different linguistic experience into the classroom. These are rich educational resources. Their parents too, given proper encouragement, can bring much to the whole school environment. The experiences of people whose languages are other than English provide an opportunity in the central task of educating for human understanding, and for the cultural empathy and exchange which are crucial for the building up and working of a happy multiracial society in Britain and the wider world. These aspects are important enough to be given proper attention in the early years when positive attitudes can be built up.

Linguistic diversity in Britain

Britain has, of course, long been a multilingual and multi-dialectal country. It took many centuries for English in its current forms and dialects to evolve from Old English, being influenced by the variety of differing languages brought by the many peoples who have made the British Isles their home. In this process, certain linguistic forms have played a dominant role, but the process of the evolution of languages and dialects is never complete.

Two historical dimensions merit discussion because of the way that they have helped structure present day attitudes. Firstly, for three to four centuries after the Norman Conquest, French was the language of the ruling classes and dominant in those educated classes closely connected to the ruling class in feudal society. It was for a long time a main language of commerce. 'English' was seen as the inferior language of the uneducated and the unschooled, spoken by freemen and peasants. It had to fight its way up culturally to achieve its own full self-conscious recognition by the time of Shakespeare. Via the Church, of course, Latin too had a key role particularly until the Reformation. This situation had profound effects on attitudes towards the languages of the ruled, and these effects survived long after this type of linguistic dualism of rulers and ruled had gone.

Secondly, the role of the various Celtic languages (Welsh, Irish, Scots and Gaelic) and of some major dialects needs to be considered. The attitude of the ruling classes towards these languages and the peoples who spoke them was to see them as marginal and this boded ill for the development of a truly pluralistic attitude towards linguistic diversity. There were concerted attempts to eliminate various Celtic languages and given the pressures it is perhaps remarkable that they have persisted so long. Their very survival is in itself an indication of just how close and important the mother tongue is in terms of identity and culture, and of how it can provide a means of protection against a hostile or exploitative group. It makes it harder for the exploiters to understand what is going on, and provides a source of pride in the face of attempts at cultural or economic domination.

Immigration, linguistic diversity and the multi-lingual society

Various immigrant groups have brought their own languages with them to Britain over the past 150 years or so. It is worth remembering that this immigration is part of a much longer pattern of immigration involving refugees like the Huguenots and the Jews, as well as economic migrants like the Irish.

Jewish people came in the seventeenth century when the ban on them was lifted, and later their numbers were augmented by refugees. These waves of Jewish people came speaking European languages like Polish or German, as well as Yiddish, the language Jewish people had developed from their own linguistic heritage in interaction with the languages they had encountered in the diaspora. By now, Jews are largely linguistically assimilated, although they retain their culture to a greater or lesser extent, with religious Jews learning Hebrew for liturgical purposes.

The Huguenots also came to Britain in the seventeenth century and constituted a large proportion of the population. Although they brought skills that were important in the industrialisation of Britain, their linguistic influence has not been extensive. The Irish too, despite their numbers, have not much influenced English, since most of them were either English speakers or bilingual. Hostility against Irish culture and language has often scarcely been acknowledged, and only in the last twenty years have the needs of Irish people been recognised by Local Authorities, who have often been exposed to much criticism for doing any thing at all.

The ways that these groups have been treated have helped to structure both attitudes and policy making in the post-war period. There have been and continue to be differences, depending upon whether the immigrants were refugees, or economic migrants, whether they sought to come or were invited here to meet particular labour shortages, whether they came as aliens or as British citizens, but overall the record of the authorities in relation to linguistic needs has not been satisfactory.

Eastern and Southern Europeans

The war itself and its aftermath brought large numbers of refugees, mostly from Eastern Europe, including considerable numbers of Polish people as well as smaller groups from the Baltic States and the Ukraine. In addition there were people from Southern Europe, particularly Italians, and later Spanish and Portuguese. All these groups brought with them their own religious leaders and maintained contact through community networks and their own cultural centres, which were also an important resource for language maintenance. Polish people established their own network of Supplementary schools to teach Polish language and help maintain culture and identity. The fact that the community stayed rooted in their language and culture, while at the same time becoming fluent in English, may well be a significant factor in explaining why Polish children have been above average in terms of academic success.

Italian immigrants who came in the immediate post-war period augmented the Italian populations who had immigrated earlier. Many of these immigrants settled in specific towns in the Midlands and South where their labour was sought. There are still many children of Italian speaking parents, and for many of these, Italian will be the mother tongue. Links with Italy are often strong, which facilitates language maintenance, and some of them will speak dialects, a fact that teachers of children starting school need to bear in mind, and which has produced problems for providers of mother tongue facilities. A number of successful projects have, however, been run for these and other significant speakers of minority languages from Europe and elsewhere (See *The Other Languages of England: the Linguistic Minorities Project*, Routledge & Kegan Paul 1985). European Community Directives detail language rights including those pertaining to the right to instruction in the mother tongue. British Governments have invariably tried to weaken such proposals and progress in implementing them in British schools has been slow.

Black and Asian people

When immigration in the post Second World War period is referred to, this is often a coded way of talking about black or 'coloured' immigration. This is a reflection of the racism in society, for statistically those immigrants who originate from the countries that are classified as 'New Commonwealth and Pakistan' (NCP) are not so large a majority as the discourse of many politicians and much of the mass media would suggest. It needs to be remembered that even by the nineteen seventies the majority of children of immigrants from NCP were born in Britain, and are not therefore themselves immigrants. By the nineteen nineties the majority of black and Asian *parents* of children in Nursery and infant classes are also not themselves immigrants.

These black and Asian immigrants can be grouped into categories depending on where the families originated: the Caribbean, South Asia, the Far East, Africa; although all the time it is necessary to be aware of the danger of generalisation and stereotyping.

People of Caribbean origin

Children whose parents or grandparents come from the Caribbean overwhelmingly speak English, as did the majority of their forebears who immigrated to Britain from the late forties to the late sixties, although the original immigrants from the Caribbean often spoke a form of Creole or Patois that some linguists have distinguished as a separate language. Some spoke a French or Spanish based Creole, and these, of course, were foreign language speakers. Immigrants who used the Creole or a dialect at home, could also communicate in Standard English. There are, however, factors concerning Creole retentions and the influence of 'British Black English' which can have a bearing on the speech and writing of young children in nursery and infant classes.

People of South Asian origin

The principal linguistic groups emanating from South Asia are Panjabi, Gujerati and Bengali. The majority of these speakers came direct from the Indian sub-continent, although an appreciable number came from East Africa. Panjabi is the main language spoken in the Punjab, a region of the sub-continent that was divided after partition when the separate states of Indian and Pakistan were set up. In addition to Muslims and Hindus displaced by the new borders there was a large population of Sikhs. Many Panjabi speakers immigrated to Britain in the nineteen fifties and early sixties. Sikhs, Muslims and Hindus speak differing varieties of Panjabi relating to the district in the Punjab that their families originate from. Literacy for Panjabi speaking Sikhs and Hindus has usually been in Panjabi, whilst for Panjabi speaking Muslims literacy is likely to be in Urdu. The differences in scripts as well as spoken language are, of course, of importance to the teacher of young children particularly when beginning writing. A detailed account of the relationships between these languages in their spoken and written forms, as it affects speakers in Britain is to be found in *The Other Languages of England: the Linguistic Minorities Project* (op. cit.). Speakers from the Indian sub-continent will often be able to communicate in Hindi/Urdu, almost always in addition to their mother tongue. Most Pakistanis speak a variety or dialect of Panjabi, although culturally they are distinct from the Indians, especially as most of them are Muslims. In many parts of the country, Panjabi community organisations, often based around places of worship, are strong, and linked to Supplementary Schooling including mother tongue provision.

Gujerati speakers have their linguistic roots in the province of Gujerat on the North-Western coast of Indian next to Pakistan. Gujerati speakers also formed a large proportion of the East African Asians, descendants of indentured labourers who had been taken in the nineteenth century to British East African territories for specific purposes like building the railways. They had stayed on as traders and small businessmen, only leaving when home rule brought pressures for Africanisation in these States. They are usually fluent in English and wish to being up their children bilingually, while Gujerati speakers from the Province itself would not usually have become fluent in English until they came to Britain. Gujerati speakers, who are often engaged in the retail trade, are found throughout Britain.

It is important to remember that linguistically the Indian sub-continent is very diverse and large provinces often contain many closely related languages and dialects. The majority of Bengali speakers use a dialect, called Sylheti, which many linguists would claim as a separate language. These immigrants came from the Sylhet district of Bangladesh, the vast majority of them working in the textile industry, often in bad conditions. Some Bangladeshis from Chittagong and other districts run Indian restaurants and are more prosperous than those in the textile industry, but in general, of all the Asian groups Bangladeshis are the worst off economically. They are later arrivals, coming in the sixties, with dependants arriving later. Some surveys have found that children of Bangladeshi origin are underachieving in schools. Parents, especially mothers, are less likely to speak fluent English than those of other groups and special care needs to be taken with messages and letters home, where translation will often be necessary.

All the languages from the sub-continent, along with the European languages discussed so far, belong to the Indo-European family of languages. They have common origins and although they do not all have the same written scripts they have similar grammatical structures, and much of the vocabulary in these greatly varied languages can be traced to common roots. This has educational implications in that it is easier to move from one Indo-European language to another, as much of the structure of the language will be the same, however different the language may look or sound.

Figure 1 shows the main languages to be found in nursery and infant schools and the language groups to which they are considered to belong. Further detailed information can be obtained from the *Catalogue of Languages Spoken by ILEA Pupils* (Fourth Edition October 1987).

Figure 1   A table of languages represented in some nursery and infant classrooms

---

1. INDO-EUROPEAN LANGUAGES

Germanic – includes English
Latin – includes French, Italian, Spanish, Portuguese
Celtic – Welsh, Scots Gaelic, Irish
Slavonic – includes Polish
Greek
Balto-Slavonic – Lithuanian, Latvian
Indo-Iranian (a) *Sanskrit Group* – includes Romany, Hindi/Urdu, Panjabi,
                Gujerati, Bengali/Sylheti
              (b) *Iranian Group* – includes Kurdish

2. SINO-TIBETAN LANGUAGES

Chinese

3. NIGER-CONGO LANGUAGES

Western Sudanic (various West African Languages)

4. AFRO-ASIATIC OR HAMITO-SEMITIC

Semitic – includes Arabic
Cushitic – includes Somali

5. ALTAIC

Turkish

People of Chinese origin

Although some communities were established earlier, most people of Chinese origin came from Hong Kong in the nineteen sixties and seventies. There are also some people of other Far Eastern backgrounds. Most speak varieties of Cantonese, a distinct spoken form of Chinese, although there are also other Chinese languages and dialects spoken. In addition many refugees from Vietnam are ethnic Chinese, also speaking forms of Cantonese. Chinese and other Far Eastern languages are tonal based and markedly different in logic and structure from Indo-European languages.

People of African origin

African languages are represented in Britain, though communities as such are usually quite small. In parts of London there are substantial numbers of speakers of West African languages. Some of these come for reasons of study, stay for a number of years, and then return to their countries of origin. Most of these come from Nigeria or Ghana, and often their children are looked after by others, following traditional West African practice, and teachers need to be aware of the implications this can have. The structures of languages will vary depending on what region they come from. The majority of immigrants from Africa and their children speak fluent English.

People of Turkish and Greek origin

Turkish, an Altaic language, has its own particular structures and vocabulary, making, as for Chinese, cross-language learning more challenging. Significant numbers of Turkish speakers are to be found especially in North East London. In the Inner London Education Authority (ILEA) language surveys of the early nineteen eighties, Turkish speakers in inner London schools were only outnumbered by Bengali speakers among the minority languages. People of Turkish origin come mostly from Cyprus, a former British colony. The larger immigrant group coming from Cyprus were Greek speakers. Again, these have settled in London mostly in the North East boroughs. Greek is an Indo-European language, but has its own alphabet.

In the late eighties, a number of Kurdish refugees from the Eastern part of Turkey and Iraq has also arrived, settling again mostly in North East London. They speak Kurdish, an Indo-European language which is, however, written in a variation of the Arabic script. In the current political situation, arrival of children of refugee origin, whose language differences are compounded by other factors, is always a possibility.

Bilingual factors

It has been established that bi-lingualism in itself is a positive advantage to young children. However some young children, from for instance South Asian backgrounds, could be facing three different languages. Research shows that there is no problem if children have already acquired the basic structures in their first language. Problems arise when a child has only a partial command of several languages. There are powerful arguments here for effective mother tongue teaching and maintenance especially in the years before statutory school age. Children will be exposed to the home language in their community and their relationships with their parents, and even more so with their grandparents, will be damaged if they do not have command of the appropriate languages.

It is worth noting here that throughout the Indian Education System, for instance, policy is that up to eight years old children are taught in their mother tongue; at eight they also learn Hindi, and at or before secondary stage they learn English as a third language. There is an expectation of needing more than one language as an educated person. This approach is of course parallelled in many European nations too, but not in English speaking countries!

Language and power

Perceptions of language helped to structure the thinking of English people in their initial and subsequent contacts with peoples that they exploited and conquered. Rigid structural differentiation based on colour and culture grew up in the colonies, and in order to justify this exploitation, the dominated peoples were declared to be 'inherently' inferior in one way or another, which always resulted in downgrading of their languages. This racism differed in degree and kind from the ethnocentrism which is to be found in most societies, shown in the mutual dislike between different nations. Racism has led to a body of literature in which claims about the intellectual and moral superiority of the white 'race' are made, which are only in recent years being fully repudiated. Overt racist organisations, nevertheless, still repeat this kind of 'theory'. In this context, academic racism, such as that of Jensen (discussed in Edwards, 1979) purporting the intellectual inferiority of black children, can have serious effects by providing a spurious rationale for avowedly racist right-wing groups.

However, irrespective of the historical legacy, racism is reproduced in current British society, as a result of an economic system that produces competition for scarce resources. Racial discrimination is far from eliminated despite being illegal, and continues to affect every person either as victim or perpetrator. For white people, the historical legacy of racism is still part of the culture, reflected through the mass media, in literature, customs, expressions and jokes. It is further reproduced by the way that discrimination is perpetuated. Young children are affected by the ideological dimension reflected in the attitudes of adults, which affect the children's perceptions and behaviour, as Milner (1975 and 1983) has shown. If parents or carers are subjects of discrimination in housing or employment, this also will, at the least, affect the sense of well-being of the children, however much adults attempt to protect them.

We are all caught up on the continuum of racism. The only viable position is an anti-racist one which acknowledges the ideological influences and recognises that everyone in one way or another is involved in discriminatory structures, and needs to take a stand against racism to dismantle both racist structures and racist attitudes.

Where language is concerned, racism and ethnocentrism work in parallel, so that the hierarchy of treatment of different groups gets reflected in attitudes taken towards the various languages. Thus non-European languages are invariably seen as implicitly inferior, not sought after, ignored or undervalued even where they have an established literature and are spoken by millions of people. The National Curriculum and the 1988 Education Reform Act have driven community languages, which constitute the mother tongues for the significant groups that have been discussed, to the edge of the curriculum or even off it.

Mullard (1982) has characterised responses since 1960 in a way which has been taken up in a number of Local Authority Equal Opportunities Policies on 'race'. *Assimilation* characterised the period when all that was expected was that non-English speakers would be taught English, and all would be well. In fact it may have never been 'well', even before this time, for substantial numbers of children from white minority groups, or from some working class backgrounds; but once the children concerned could be identified by their 'colour' it was hard to disguise the problem. Children at this time were segregated if they did not speak English, usually into separate classes or units, or even separate schools, with all the bad effects that had in encouraging stereotypes and hampering the development of healthy social relationships across racial boundaries.

It was in the late sixties, Mullard (1982) claims, that the deficiencies of an Assimilationist approach became clear and new policies which could be described as *Integrationist* were tried. The idea that all children could or should be culturally 'the same' was abandoned, and it was recognised that while there should be common citizenship and an agreed legal framework, there should also be freedom for people to retain their language and customs. By the seventies Integration had given way to *Cultural Pluralism* as the dominant paradigm. More stress was given to cultural diversity, and it was at this time that ideas of education for a multicultural society came into their own.

Unfortunately, while it has been well-intentioned, multicultural education has not delivered equality of opportunity in relation to 'race'. It is true that it was only really attempted in a thorough-going way in a few schools, and by a few Local Education Authorities, and even now multicultural initiatives are still only just reaching some schools in 'all-white' areas. However, the most that multicultural education can do is to raise awareness about cultural difference, help pupils in the appreciation of cultural diversity, and perhaps remove some of the worst stigmas applied to second language speakers. Multiculturalism has been analysed by a number of other writers, such as Stone (1981) who described its deficiencies.

The problem with multiculturalism was that it did not acknowledge that the fundamental issue was a structural one, historically produced and reproduced by persistent racism, as has been seen above. More recently attention has been drawn to the way that children, as well as being disadvantaged, can suffer harassment in or on the way to school (as revealed by the Commission for Racial Equality in *Learning in Terror: A survey of racial harassment in schools and colleges*, 1988). The morale of parents and carers of young children is undermined by discrimination and harassment and this too will affect the children themselves, however subtly. The issue is not just one of cultural exchange, important though that is in itself. True multicultural exchange cannot take place when one group is held in a consistently inferior position to the other. The issue is about relative power. In relation to access to almost any area of power in the economic or political fields, Black and Asian people still start at a disadvantage compared to white people, though hierarchy and differential access to power operate within the white group too.

Racism is institutionalised in all areas of society. It occurs whenever rules and practices operate to exclude Black or Asian people or treat them in an inferior way to white people, even though this may be in no way intended. For example, in a nursery to which applications have to be made by letter or on forms requiring fluent English, the fact that this may exclude many families may not in the first place have been apparent to those who made this rule. Examples are seldom so explicit, since the Race Relations Act (1976) outlaws discrimination in relation to admissions to schooling, but cases of a more subtle kind are myriad. The image or style of the pre-school facility, the fact that black people cannot even get to hear about it, the dress requirements, staff attitudes, the innuendoes concerning languages other than English, are more likely to constitute the problem. Institutional practices exist despite and beyond the attitudes of the individuals concerned. They are persistent and their removal is difficult.

In order to try to combat racism in society and in the educational system, including pre-school education, some Local Authorities and schools have adopted anti-racist policies in the attempt to provide a context for cultural and linguistic awareness and sharing. The barriers to the unity of humankind and to the justice which is the foundation of equality of opportunity, are not the cultural or linguistic differences in themselves but the racist and other discriminatory structures of society. Unfortunately, such initiatives have been attacked, and any mistakes in their implementation seized on to inflame prejudice. Those ignorant of research and theory have, for instance, ridiculed the learning of nursery rhymes in South Asian languages.

The National Curriculum does in places acknowledge cultural diversity, but in defining 'English' as 'Language', effectively marginalises community languages and mother tongues. Also by crowding the curriculum with the statutory subjects, it makes it harder for even the enthusiastic teacher to find time for mother tongue teaching as a separate item. Mother tongues can be used before the statutory National Curriculum age but their use in more than a support role has been discouraged, both for delivery of the National Curriculum and, except in special situations, for testing. The way Modern Languages have been classified at Secondary level will also have a bad effect on the maintenance of key mother tongues lower down the education system.

Nonetheless, at Nursery and pre-school levels some flexibility remains. It is easier to create and maintain a multi-lingual atmosphere where all tongues are welcomed and can be developed. Enlightened teachers have realised how important it it to put themselves in the place of the child who does not speak English, or who has a mother tongue that is not English. Since the nineteen sixties, far-sighted nursery and infant teachers have sought to encourage mother tongues, some learning the languages themselves. Awareness of the importance of mother tongue in terms of competence in the first language being a good foundation for competence in the second, is now widespread among nursery and infant teachers. Classes, particularly in multi-lingual areas, often reflect this multi-lingualism. There is a greater realisation, at least among teachers and under-fives workers, that we live in a shrinking world.

This was graphically brought home to me on a trip to Bangladesh where, in the heart of the countryside, I met Bangladeshi children speaking English with rich Yorkshire accents. There is a need to prepare children for a future that may take some of them back to their family's country of origin, where the development of their mother tongue competence is crucial.

Because of the insidious nature of racism, there is a need to be especially watchful. The Nursery and Infant class teacher is in the forefront of the formation of attitudes to language, in children and in parents, as an opportunity and a challenge.

CHAPTER 2

Varieties of English

Linda Thomas and Shân Wareing

Teachers who are involved in developing a child's English need to give some thought to linguistic variation within English itself and the mythology surrounding the prestige form. The issue of Standard English as opposed to other varieties of English can perhaps be compared to one of those visual brain twisters – the white shape with a black surround that could be two human profiles, or could be a vase. You can switch from seeing one to seeing the other, but you cannot see both simultaneously. Standard English is the variety of English commonly referred to as 'correct English', 'accurate English', 'grammatical English'. To thus perceive Standard English necessitates all other varieties of English being perceived as 'wrong', 'ungrammatical', 'uneducated', 'substandard'. This is one possible view of the arrangement of shapes.The alternate view is to see 'English' as being an umbrella term which covers many varieties of the language, and Standard English as one of these varieties, differentiated from other varieties by the contexts in which it is used and by the group of speakers who use it, but not by linguistic regularity or superiority. Both views are held, and are mutually exclusive. In this chapter we will be stating the case for the latter.

A cursory glance at the history of the rise of the variety known as Standard English will help put this view into perspective. Standard English emerged from the Middle English Dialect spoken in the South East Midland area of England for a variety of historical reasons. The Oxford-Cambridge-London triangle was already a centre for trade and commerce, learning, Government and the Church, so that the variety of that region was being used in contexts that other regional varieties of English were not. (There was considerable variation in the types of English being used throughout England at this time, not to mention the other indigenous languages such as Scots and Welsh).

With William Caxton's development of the English printing press, on which he printed his first book in 1475, the South-East Midland variety of English which he selected also gained further status. Owing to academic and literary usages of the prestige form and its use in other official and commercial contexts, the Modern English descendant of Caxton's South-East Midland dialect acquired a prestige which far exceeded that of any other British variety of the English language. This led to its widespread imposition throughout the British Isles, and, as a result of trade and military power, to its being recognized as a high status language form throughout the world. (For detailed accounts see Leith, 1983; Milroy and Milroy, 1985). For many people, 'Standard British English' and 'English' are synonomous.

The cost of this high status language variety has been the stigmatisation of the other regional and ethnic varieties of English. Another factor in this equation is literacy, since, for the reasons discussed above, the language of literacy is Standard English. The prestige that attaches to literacy confers added status on the standard dialect. The dialect of literacy, thus seen as the 'correct' form, is then demanded in speech as well as in writing.

Similarly, as a high status language used world-wide, the process of stigmatisation has also affected languages other than English, especially those languages dominated by English as a result of military imperialism (for example, from the continent of Africa and the sub-continent of India). The same language-prejudice which led to the marginalisation and virtual disappearance of the other indigenous languages of Britain (Scots, Scottish Gaelic, Irish Gaelic, Cornish, Welsh) is apparent in attitudes to the current other languages of Britain.

There is an issue here of power. World languages such as English and French are languages of power, and are perceived as 'real' languages (with English as the front runner if the opinion of *The Daily Mail* of 14.11.1991: Headline 'Europe needs plain English', is anything to go by). Non-power languages are not perceived as 'real' languages in the same way that non-power dialects are not perceived as 'real' English. We need to be aware of whether our attitudes to languages and language varieties are reflections of our attitudes to their speakers.

Let us look at this point at what we mean by varieties of English apart from Standard English. Variation in English can be linked with geographic diversity, socio-economic class status, and ethnic affiliation. In each case, it is the varieties used by groups that have low social status in British society that are stigmatised. We have already said that it was the dialect of the South-East Midlands which emerged as the standard form of English. Thus the dialects spoken in the rest of England diminished in status, to the extent that they came to be regarded as used only by uneducated speakers and dismissed as simply 'wrong'. Instead of being regarded as historical accident, the standard form came to be, and still is, regarded as inherently superior.

The national press abounds with the views of self-appointed language censors, such as John Rae, the former headteacher of Westminister School, who writes:

> I thought it was correct to write 'we were' and incorrect to write 'we was'... I thought it was a question of grammar or, if you do not like that word, of logic. You cannot use the singular form of the verb with a plural pronoun. (John Rae, in *The Evening Standard*, 17.11.1983)

All language varieties have grammar – that is, a set of underlying laws that govern, amongst other things, the word order and the inflections which tell you, again amongst other things, if an action is past or present (I paint vs. I paint*ed*), who is doing it (I paint vs. she paint*s* in Standard English). Without grammar, instead of comprehensible utterances we would have word salads, as you would if you cut words out of a newspaper and flung them in the air – no order, no sense. John Rae is not criticizing varieties of English which have 'no grammar', or 'incorrect grammar', but ones which have a grammatical system which has a limited number of systematic differences from the Standard English which is the variety he uses. And contradicting his charge of 'illogical', an analysis of many non-standard forms reveals more 'logical' systems than Standard English possesses. For example, consider the following typical non-standard paradigm of the verb 'to go', in contrast to the standard form:

Typical non-standard paradigm				*Standard paradigm*			
I	goes	we	goes	I		go	we	go
you	goes	you	goes	you		go	you	go
s/he, it	goes	they	goes	s/he, it	goes	they	go

(Cheshire 1982a)

It is the standard paradigm that has the wayward inflection in it: the totally regular non-standard paradigm, if judged on the basis of regularity, is surely the more logical. The standard paradigm also disproves John Rae's claim that you 'cannot use a singular form of the verb with a plural pronoun' – how does such an argument account for 'I go' and 'they go', or indeed 'you are' addressed to one person, and 'you are' addressed to a roomful of people? To attempt to claim linguistic superiority for the standard form of English on the grounds of logic is doomed from the outset.

A further instance of this is in general attitudes towards the common non-standard form of multiple negation. Prescriptivists suggest that more than one negative form in utterances such as 'I ain't got none' rationally communicates a positive not a negative (so the meaning is really 'I have got some'). Whilst the prescriptivist interpretation is debatable (for instance, we know of no-one who interprets Mick Jagger's line 'I can't get no satisfaction' as meaning that he can) we would also point out that the accusation of illogicality is not levelled at languages such as Spanish, where multiple negation is standard.

The criterion of logic was also invoked when assessing the language development of Black English Vernacular speakers in New York (Labov, 1969). Labov looked at the accusations of illogicality which had been levelled at these speakers with regard to such features as multiple negation, and copula deletion. Copula deletion refers to the non-appearance of the relevant form of the verb 'to be ' in utterances such as 'They mine' ('They are mine' in standard English). Labov explains that deletion:

> . . . is not the result of erratic or illogical behaviour: it follows the same regular rules as standard English contraction. Wherever standard English can contract, Negro (sic) children use either the contracted form or (more commonly) the deleted zero form. Thus 'They mine' corresponds to standard 'They're mine' not to the full form 'They are mine'. On the other hand, no such deletion is possible in positions where standard English cannot contract: just as one cannot say 'That's what they're' in standard English, 'That's what they' is equally impossible in the vernacular . . . (p. 203)

Relevant detailed studies of British Black English varieties are those of Sutcliffe, 1982; Edwards, 1986, Hewitt, 1986.

The significance of the above issues to English in the classroom is that the majority of children in Britain do not have Standard English as their home variety, and many do not have any variety of English as a first language. This is clearly a matter of prime importance for teachers involved in English teaching at every level in the education system. Because the teaching of literacy is one of the fundamental concerns of institutionalised education, the English that teachers are primarily concerned with developing is Standard English. It is, however, essential to take into account that the child in the classroom may have a regional non-standard variety of English as their first form of language, or, where English is a second language, their first form of English.

The importance of linguistic awareness when dealing with non-standard dialects in the classroom has been demonstrated by Cheshire's (1982b) work on Reading school children. Uninformed alteration of features of Reading English to Standard English produced linguistic confusion which persisted in some cases into secondary school. Children did not have the familiarity with Standard English to understand the motivation for the teacher's 'correction' of the non-standard Reading dialect, with the result that one dialect interfered with the other, and pupils' written language contained forms which were not appropriate to either dialect. The implication of this research for the teacher of young children is clear: imposition of unfamiliar forms at too early a stage may lead to confusion and lack of confidence in both oral and written language.

The most recent guidance on the teaching of English appeared in the form of the Cox Report (1989) and subsequent National Curriculum guidelines. Whilst making reference to the issue of social and regional variation in English, this government-commissioned material concentrated on the transmission of the standard form. It permitted tolerance of non-standard forms, to the extent that it did not recommend the immediate and unconditional replacement of dialectal forms of English with Standard English forms in children's speech from the moment they enter the classroom. However, Cox's emphasis on the use of Standard English speech in the public domain maintains its position of superiority whilst confirming the inferior status of non-standard forms, which are seen as appropriate only in informal or domestic situations. This leads us back to the question of whose English we are teaching and confirming in the classroom.

Sociolinguists such as Peter Trudgill (1975 for instance), hold the position that not only is awareness of language variation important in the teaching of English but that Standard English should be taught for what it is: that is, another, but not superior, dialect of English.

While young children often have an implicit awareness of language variation at a very early age (and can, for instance, easily distinguish

East Enders from *Neighbours* or *Coronation Street*), explicit teaching may not be needed in the Infant School. Recognition where appropriate of the differences between the language varieties of children, or between them and the teacher, and respect for all varieties of language, is probably sufficient at this stage.

We have set out in brief the reasons for the development of Standard English, and illustrated the fact that other varieties of English might make at least equal claim to logic and regularity. We have also pointed out that there is a political history to the ascension of Standard English as a major language form, which is directly connected to the low status of indigenous languages of colonised countries and to the low status of the non-standard forms of English which are used primarily by low socio-economic groups. How language variation is dealt with by individual teachers in individual classes is far from simple and the debate is far from closed. We hope we have clarified at least some of the issues at stake, so that the debate may continue productively.

CHAPTER 3

Language and Learning in the Multi-cultural Nursery

Christine Stevenson

> If the culture of the teacher is to become part of the consciousness of the child, then the culture of the child must first be in the consciousness of the teacher. B. Bernstein (1970)

Young children make sense of their experiences through talk but it is their talk *with adults* that generally extends their understanding of that experience. Young children do not usually operate in isolation; their experiences are shared with those adults who understand and ratify the experience for children through the use of talk. Because the experience is shared the talk has meaning for children. They need conceptual understanding to give words their meaning which is gained through experience. Thus, it must follow that experience shared with adults, in the sense of having common understanding of that experience, must promote conceptual understanding for children. The following transcript demonstrates this point. It records a discussion that took place between a nursery teacher and a child aged 4 years 3 months following a project based around the book called *We're Going on a Bear Hunt* by Michael Rosen (1989). The project had culminated in a 'bear hunt' for the nursery class in a local wood and a corresponding bear hunt area had been set up in the outside play area of the nursery.

Child: Can I draw a story of the 'bear hunt'?
Teacher: Of course.
Child: I've drawn the grass; I've drawn the trees and the wood; I've drawn the cave and the bear. Have I missed anything out? (After drawing, contemplates).
Teacher: The mud?
Child: Oh yes, the mud. (Draws the mud).
Teacher: Let's get the book now and see if you have everything.

	(Looks through book with child). Your drawing looks like a map.
Child:	What's a map?
Teacher:	A map is where you show where everything is so that anyone can go there and find the trees in the wood, the grass and the cave with the bear. (The teacher writes under each drawing as she talks naming the drawings 'wood', 'mud' etc).
Child:	That's good. Now I can use my map to go on a bear hunt. (Takes the 'map' outside and uses it in the outside play area).

The transcript reveals a common understanding of, in this instance, the bear hunt, between teacher and child. This has enabled the teacher to introduce a new word 'map' and an idea of what the word means appropriate to the child's level of understanding which he is then able to reinforce through experience.

It becomes evident that, where children have experience in which the teacher/adult plays no part or of which she has little or no understanding, it will be difficult for her to extend the conceptual understanding of that experience for children.

How important is this? What is the relevance for the teacher in the multi-cultural nursery? It might be argued that the role played by the teacher in extending children's understanding, as shown in the above transcript, exemplifies the aims of education. Holding on to this role can often be difficult for the teacher in the welter of other matters that crowd into a busy school day. Yet to understand how young children learn and how she can best support that learning is probably the most important part of a teacher's expertise. Explanations in text books designed for teachers often gloss over difficulties or are encased in jargon and hard to unravel. In this chapter I shall attempt to clarify the place of language in children's learning before moving on to how this fits into the context of the multi-cultural nursery.

Very young children begin to make contact with their world by a process of active exploration. Their environment is a mêlée of sights and noises which they first register in immediate terms – reiterating sounds heard and playing with them, finding out which sound fits in and draws the appropriate response from other people. That every object has a name is a realisation that children will come to at about the age of two years. Adults, however, think of the word as representing the object; children rather perceive the word as the property or an attribute of the object. For instance, Vygotsky (1986), tells of simple experiments that show:

how pre-school children 'explain' the name of objects by their attributes. According to them, an animal is called 'cow' because it has horns, 'calf' because its horns are still small, 'dog' because it is small and has no horns; an object is called 'car' because it is not an animal. When asked whether one could interchange the name of objects, for instance, call a cow 'ink' and ink 'cow', children will answer no, 'because ink is used for writing, and the cow gives milk'. (pp. 222/3)

By the same token, the word 'cup' is a word in English that denotes a common, everyday object. The word actually used is arbitrary for we might call it a 'sut' or a 'tep', indeed anything at all provided we have a shared understanding of what is meant when we speak of it. The child of nursery age will have no notion of this arbitrary nature of language. The word meaning is tied into the interpretation given to it by the child in the social context that it is first learned. It is that social and cultural experience that is bound up in the child's understanding of a word and gives it its meaning.

Consider the meanings associated with the following statement for two children – one from an English Protestant background, the other from an Indian Hindu background:

The car came round the corner and drove fast towards the cow standing in the middle of the road.

Each child will interpret the sentence differently, we might argue, according to the cultural significance of the word 'cow', for the Indian Hindu child will have grown up with an understanding of a cow as a sacred animal to be revered and protected. Thus we can see that the child will have a conceptual understanding which is not only generally attributed to a word but is also representative of the layers of associations and meanings that are attached to the idea of, in this instance, what a cow is. The child will have gained this interpretation not in any passive way but actively in the everyday life that she leads. As Vygotsky (1986) describes:

In the beginning was the deed. The word was not the beginning – action was there first; it is the end of development crowning the deed. (p. 255)

The words that we use are rooted in the culture in which we develop. As Heller (1987) suggests:

[For members of an ethnic group] shared experience forms the basis of a shared way of looking at the world; through interaction they jointly construct ways of making sense of experience. These ways of making sense of experience, these beliefs, assumptions and expectations about the world and how it works underlie what we think of as culture. (p. 184)

For a group to feel cultural identity the members will share ownership of cultural features that define and characterise the group. These will operate in a functional and symbolic manner as, for instance, in the language used. Ferdman (1990) tells how, 'for many Puerto Ricans in the United States, the Spanish language is not just a means of communication; it also represents their identification as Latinos and their difference from the majority culture'. (p. 190). The view of the wider society as to whether such cultural features are seen as positive or negative will influence the way in which the group itself views these features.

But children, certainly at the time of entering the nursery class, will use words with only a partial conceptual understanding and will categorise aspects of their world in response to visual stimuli without real understanding and discrimination. For example, the child might regard all large objects as being heavier than small objects. Children gain conceptual understanding as they learn more about themselves and their environment. The nature of their experience will dictate the kinds of understanding gained as can be seen in Mead's study (1971) of Manus children living in the Admiralty Islands off New Guinea, who gain an early understanding of the concept of weight compared to European children. Manus children live with their families in villages built on stilts over water where everything has to be pulled up into the huts and in so doing these children learn that shape does not necessarily indicate weight. This is indicative of the way in which cultural background influences their development.

Words are acquired in a context that is meaningful for the children and as children develop so too will word meanings evolve through the relationship which words have to their thinking. Vygotsky (1986) is clear on this point – that thought comes into being through words so that as thought flows, develops and grows, connections are made and problems solved with the use of spoken words. How does this actually work? He describes how children acquire speech in two ways or 'aspects', each operative at the same time:

(1)   through meaning (internal)
(2)   through the phonetic (external).

The second aspect is obvious in that it is easily observed and recorded that young children first use one word before learning to connect two or three words, then proceed to use of simple sentences before more complex sentences and, ultimately, are able to speak coherently.

The first aspect is not so obvious to observe and record in children even though this is developing at the same time as the external phonetic aspect. Children have a very vague conceptual understanding of a word at first because of their limited experience and their use of the word might suggest an understanding that they do not yet have. As their conceptual understanding develops so they are able to use words which more aptly describe what they understand. These two aspects of speech acquisition graphically encapsulate how the child develops from whole to parts in terms of refining meaning and from parts to whole in terms of extending external phonetic speech.

At the same time and not by co-incidence, Vygotsky (1986) says, children initially use 'speech' out loud to describe for themselves what is happening around them in order to make sense of their experience. This so-called 'egocentric' speech is bound up in social speech for others at this stage. As children develop, the speech for themselves moves inward to become thought. This becomes possible as children learn to differentiate between speech for others and speech for themselves through the talk generated by social interaction and shared experiences.

In order to be a good learning environment, the nursery classroom has to be representative of the social world of children and support their ways of making sense of their world. The pendulum of educational thinking swings between the model of child-centred 'discovery' learning and the model of didactic imposition of facts by teacher on child. How are teachers to resolve this dilemma? Most teachers know that a delicate balance exists between these two models. Children learn by testing their hypotheses in the environment through experience. If the problem is insurmountable they fall back or misinterpret what is needed to solve the problem. Telling the child the answer (however well intentioned) may well conflict with the complex network of acquiring knowledge and thus cause confusion, possibly blocking further creative exploration. The child is inhibited in this case by the adult intervention.

Vygotsky (1986) offers us a way of promoting a child's learning by use of a key term which he calls the 'zone of proximal development'. He presents the case of children solving their own problems thus indicating a measurable level of development, but gaining a part picture only. When children are presented with problems too difficult to manage alone Vygotsky shows that, with assistance, they can resolve those problems. The opening transcript in this chapter is an example. Some children were found by Vygotsky (1986) to have achieved levels in solving problems in collaboration far beyond what might have been expected and relative to those of other children.

> The discrepancy between a child's actual age and the level he reaches in solving problems with assistance indicates the zone of his proximal development . . . and, with assistance, every child can do more than he can by himself – though only within the limits set by the state of his development. (p. 187)

This, of course, sounds all very fine, intervening appropriately at the right time, but how? A nursery school teacher, Margaret Revell explained recently

> Get inside a child's head so you know where a child is by listening to what the child has to say, how it responds, how it reacts. Many children change when you get inside their heads and find out what interests them. Before that they don't have ownership of what goes on. You can't give ownership to them unless you know them. You can't know them unless you get inside their heads and share experiences.

Such experiences shared by a teacher with children are vividly described by Vivian Gussin Paley (1981) when she says that she searches 'for the child's point of view with which I can help him take a step further' and 'the teacher must help the child see how one thing he knows relates to other things he knows'. (p. 213)

Two conversations with children are recorded by Paley, eight months apart, which clearly demonstrate the children's developing perspectives about, in this case, apples and the implications of eating them. It was set in the context of a story told to the children about two rabbits warned by an older rabbit that eating apples from a certain tree means a fox will get them. The rabbits run out of carrots and are given apples from the forbidden tree by a friendly serpent who then saves them from the fox.

> *Conversation One*:
> Teacher: Why did the old rabbit think the fox would get the bunnies if they ate an apple?
> Wally: He owned the apples.
> Eddie: The fox liked apples and he thought they would steal them.
> Teacher: What if there were no apple tree? Would he stil try to eat the bunnies?

Wally: It wouldn't make any sense to say it if the apple tree wasn't there.

Eddie: He didn't want to share the apples.

Wally: If they ate it and the fox saw it, he could get them. Here's a good trick. The fox invited them for dinner and if they ate one apple he could eat them up.

Teacher: Would the fox eat the bunnies because they were eating his apples?

Wally: It must be. If it isn't that, what else could it be? (p. 191)

Here, Wally and Eddie cannot make any connections between the fox and bunnies besides the warning words in the story – that the fox will eat them if they eat the apples. In order to support this idea they decide that the fox must own the tree even though this is not known.

Conversation Two: (After re-reading the story 8 months later).

Teacher: Why did the old rabbit think the fox would get the bunnies if they ate the apples?

Lisa: It's the fox's apple tree and he doesn't want anyone to touch it.

Teacher: How do you know it's the fox's apple tree?

Lisa: The fox growed the tree when he moved there. It takes a long time for apples to grow so he didn't want anyone to touch his tree.

Wally: Foxes like to eat bunnies and also it takes a long time to grow the tree.

Teacher: Would the fox get the bunnies because they were eating the apples?

Wally: He might still try to keep all the apples to himself.

Teacher: What if the bunnies hadn't eaten the apples?

Earl: Maybe they couldn't reach them.

Wally: Well, he still might have tried to eat them because foxes in the forest, if there's any rabbits around, they do eat them.

Deana: Foxes like to eat rabbits best of all.

Fred: If the bunnies can't reach the apples then what if the fox doesn't get them?

Deana: He doesn't want the apples. He wants the bunnies.

Wally: He'll just keep chasing the rabbits until one day he gets them.

Kim: If it's winter and the apples are gone he'll be hungry so then he'll keep chasing them even more.

Wally: Here would be a good trick! The fox takes out all the carrots so they can't eat carrots. Then the bunnies have to come to his apple tree where he's hiding. Then he can jump on them. It's like a trap. (pp. 192/3)

Now the children have developed an awareness of the reality of foxes eating bunnies with or without apples. A better perspective has been gained of the role of the apples.

Teachers have to leave behind their pre-conceived assumptions about children as they are listening to them. They need to be receptive as to what response is most appropriate in order to enable children to solve problems, providing answers that increasingly allow children to refine their conceptual understanding. As Paley (1988) suggests:

> When I care more about what the children say and think about than my own conventionality, those are the times I sense the beat and hear the unspoken lines. (p. vii)

So how does all this fit into the context of the multi-cultural nursery, with the extra difficulties presented in communicating with children using first languages other than English? There can be no doubt, as evidenced by research, of the value of mother tongue teaching for English as a Second Language (E.S.L.) learners, most particularly for its social, emotional and motivational effects and most probably for cognitive effects also. However, one has to be realistic. Nursery school teachers are most likely to be indigenous, mono-lingual English speakers with, if they are lucky, some adult language support for the children, in addition to possible support from other children sharing the same first languages. Children's degree of proficiency will vary, both in English and in their first language. Procedures which should effect good learning through language for *all* children are as follows:

(1) The teacher will need to do all in her power to establish to what degree the child is proficient in one, both or more languages. She may need to use support staff, parents or others as translators. The means of defining as well as achieving proficiency will need to be clearly communicated to those involved, for instance, through enabling children to talk purposefully and by listening to that talk in every language used, where possible. Children will, therefore, need to feel secure with their 'listener' in order for the teacher to gain a truer picture of their proficiency in language use. This should then form part of a comprehensive profile for each child, comprising elements likely to have a bearing on a child's level of conceptual understanding:

   (a) the family and home circumstances – with home visits where possible;

(b) spoken language abilities (not necessarily representative of a child's understanding);

(c) the child's interests;

(d) linguistic provision – current and retrospective, for instance, stories heard, libraries used;

(e) social circle – how wide?

(f) outings made – local and further afield;

(g) religion.

and so on; everything, in fact, that can be gleaned to give the teacher an understanding of the children and where they are in their thinking.

The children, as well as their families, will be a major and ongoing source of information both individually and in the class setting. The diversity of such shared experiences will become a source of interest for all the children.

(2) Of considerable concern in gathering material for this paper was the evidence of nursery teachers reporting how E.S.L. children and their families perceived their first language negatively in most cases. (This did not apply to European languages which generally had a high profile). Comments commonly reported were parents' strong assertions that only English was spoken at home which was patently untrue in some cases, as one or even both parents could barely speak English. However, this was indicative of what was perceived to be necessary in the education of their children, as parents also wanted English only to be the medium for teaching in school.

Thus a clear priority establishes itself – that of asserting the positive benefits of the child's first language in the eyes of the children and their parents. Parents should understand the value of proficiency in the first language to gaining proficiency in the second language – in this case English. They could also be told of the ultimate benefits that being a balanced bilingual brings in educational terms. Given the low staff/pupil ratios in most nursery classes, it is highly important that all resources be tapped for promoting the first language of all E.S.L. speakers so that not only is speaking proficiency developed, but also the confidence of the speaker and the perceived status of their languages. Developing spoken English for all children will be equally important. The context will be a rich and structured learning environment for, as we have seen, word meanings, as opposed to just 'words' grow out of experience.

(3) One nursery teacher, Margaret Revell, said to me:

> We have to first know ourselves – it's not easy. We have to leave
> off our hang-ups otherwise we can't be receptive to the children.
> We (the staff) have to plan together for a cohesive programme
> for the children so that we all understand. Everything must be
> from the child's point of view so they don't get conflicting
> messages.

Teacher expectations of children are crucial to their achievements so it needs saying that teachers must look at themselves
and their own attitudes to the ways of life of others. If this
process is refined enough, we can say that we have a mini-culture
of our own comprising those shared experiences drawn from a
range of sources which have influenced our thinking. We
categorise more broadly in terms of cultural categories for the
reason that we categorise our world generally – to bring order to
the way we conceive a complex world.

These cultural categories and their features have to be
carefully examined for prejudice – not easy but very necessary if
we are to interact with the child's cultural level of understanding.

(4) Most important is the business of 'getting inside the childrens'
heads to find out where their thinking is' in order to extend their
conceptual understanding of their experience. The classroom
environment should incorporate as many strands of the child's
social life as is practicable so that experiences can be shared in
order to make connections between them.

To quote V. Gussin Paley (1988):

> Ideas and purposes must be processed through other children in
> social play if a child is to open up to an ever larger picture and
> determine how the pieces fit together. (p. viii)

The main medium for this process will be talk. Vygotsky (1986)
shows us how children come to conceptual understanding from
first applying a generalised hypothesis to a word based on their
experience. Further and relevant experience in combination with
discussion extends yet refines the generalised to the particular so
that a child's learning becomes truly significant and meaningful.
At the same time children are developing their linguistic cap-
abilities in phonetic terms in order to verbalise the meanings
being made. A whole word cannot just be decoded – it has to be

understood in all senses. The teacher is there to ascertain where the child is on this continuum in order to prompt the learning and set it in context – to use Gussin Paley's terms, 'stage manage' the production, with the children being the 'script-writers' and the 'actors'.

But what of the script? It seems to me that this will be a co-production between teachers and children. Plato said (Hughes, 1976) that a basic curriculum for young children should be housed in story form where the reality of children's concrete everyday experience can tap the resources of the child's inner world of thoughts through use of the imagination thus 'keeping faith, as Goethe said, with the world of things and the world of spirits equally'. (Hughes, 1976).

For our purposes nothing exists in a vacuum without reason. Knowledge has accumulated as someone or some group of people has responded somewhere to the challenge of fresh problems needing to be resolved. Thus no one group of people, however culturally defined, can claim all knowledge. Yet, in schools, knowledge – the content of what children learn – is often presented through a mono-cultural perspective and/or in an immaterial or unconnected manner. Knowledge is essentially multi-cultural and diverse in form and what better context for its presentation than the multi-cultural nursery with so many perspectives naturally present and ready to be tapped? Children need to see how connections can be made and they do this through experience and talk. The experiences provided in the nursery must make sense to children so that their talk is given purpose, valued and listened to in order to find out their starting points and growth points. In the sharing of their experiences the children will, in turn, create a culture of their own.

CHAPTER 4

Distinctive Voices – Developing Oral Language in Multilingual Classrooms

Rosemary Morgan

Why Talk?

> We are saying that it is as
> talkers, questioners, arguers,
> chatterboxes, that our pupils do
> much of their most important
> learning (Barnes *et al.*, 1969 p. 7)

The belief that children's everyday talking voices are the most versatile means they possess for making sense of the world was expressed by Barnes over two decades ago. In the past twenty years our understanding of the centrality of talk to children's learning has steadily increased and the search for the most effective ways of giving pupils a 'voice' in the classroom has gathered momentum. We are now coming to understand that children are most likely to develop into confident talkers in a climate where they:

- Feel able to make mistakes, speak tentatively and think aloud knowing that they are not being judged.
- Believe that their own language and way of speaking are respected and their opinions taken seriously.
- Experience a physical environment and organisation of learning in schools which encourages collaborative talk and the opportunities to develop this talk beyond the immediate task in hand.

Understanding the crucial role for talk in classrooms, however, is made more complex when we consider the wide diversity of languages and dialects now spoken in our schools. The 1987 I.L.E.A. survey demonstrates that 170 different languages are spoken by children in

London schools, and on a wider front the Cox Report (N.C.C. 1989) suggests that some 5% of all schools in England have a significant population of pupils for whom English is not their mother tongue. Such diversity has doubtless given many classrooms new dimensions. It may also however have raised concerns in schools as to how they can best nurture and support the talk of their bi-lingual pupils and maximize on the opportunities offered by a richer, more culturally diverse group of children.

Any account of practical ways teachers have found to welcome linguistic diversity and develop the distinctive voices of their multi-lingual pupils should perhaps begin with a timely reminder. Almost all children come to school with considerable achievement in spoken language. Frank Smith (1988) points out that children are learning language in context constantly from a very early age. By the time they start school they already have considerable knowledge of grammatical rules and register and a vocabulary of on average several thousand words, which Smith indicates continues to increase at around twenty words a day for the average five year old. Children have gained this knowledge, says Smith, from their desire to join the 'club of language users.' However, until they come to school they will have been used to learning largely from people who share their language and context. It is important for teachers of bi-lingual pupils to remember this and to understand that all young children, and especially those for whom English is their second language, may demonstrate a very different range of performance in language skills in school from those they reveal at home. So it becomes crucial to avoid stereotypes about children's abilities (Houlton, 1985) and to recognise that children may need our help in bridging the considerable gap they may experience not only between the languages spoken at home and at school, but also between the more abstract forms of school knowledge and their first-hand experiences of the world.

Westgate and Hughes (1989) indicate in their interesting research findings that teachers often fail to do this adequately and these authors note that teacher-dominated talk often leaves young children insufficient space to initiate, extend and elaborate their personal meanings. In some telling transcripts Westgate and Hughes demonstrate how teachers often appear to 'own' the interactions and allow pupils little space and opportunity to initiate or take charge of the dialogue. Children's success in a second language then will clearly require the kind of sensitive support which will motivate their desire to communicate and give them the 'space' to do so. They will already be skilled watchers and listeners, and interpreters of gestures and looks. They will also understand that spoken language is meaningful. If they are given a continuing confidence in themselves as language users their bilingualism can become a positive force in their development and a real benefit to their overall academic and intellectual progress.

Children's desire to communicate and constant search to make sense of their experiences can perhaps be demonstrated by five year old Tamima who speaks Gujerati at home. She has spent the first two months of the Autumn term in an inner London primary school. On this particular occasion thirty reception class children were busy learning a song based on the Bible story about the foolish man who built his house upon the sand. The teacher softly sang:

The rain fell down and the floods came up.

Tamima listened intently with bright-eyed enjoyment and then after a few minutes felt confident enough to join in:

The rain downstairs
In my flat ends up.

she sang cheerfully. Tamima's interpretation of the song shows us just how much linguistic expertise she has been able to bring to bear in her attempt to make sense of this new experience. Already quite competent in her first language, her contribution indicates the huge steps she has taken after only a few weeks in school and demonstrates her strong desire and determination to join this new 'club of language users.'

So how had Tamima's school supported her oral development during her crucial early days at school? If as Vygotsky tells us (1962), what children can do with help today they can do alone tomorrow, how can her school experience enable her to maximize her existing knowledge of language and build outwards? It is hard to pin down exactly what creates the kind of environment which successfully develops the skills and talents that all children bring with them. However, Tamima's school, like many others, has particularly well-thought out language policies which reflect the multicultural society in which we all live. These policies make clear reference to the importance placed on talk as a crucial means of learning. The teachers have also created an ethos within the school in which children feel comfortable and confident and where a respect for each other's languages and cultures is constantly being developed. This is reflected in the curriculum, as is the awareness of the children's needs by the adults within the organisation. Staff assume a sensitive, positive role in their attempt to scaffold and support their bilingual pupils' oral development. Throughout the school there seems to be a firm belief that children should be expected to learn for themselves, rather than by themselves.

First steps

Barrs *et al.* (1990) draw attention to the fact that bilingual pupils may have very different degrees of competence in speaking English when they come to school. For some children, English will be one of the languages spoken at home, but for others it may be far less familiar. It may be helpful to look first at the specific ways schools such as Tamima's plan for the oral development of bi-lingual pupils who are very new to English. The emphasis will remain on planning which will develop children's oracy, although it is important to remember that talking and listening, reading and writing are all closely related and development in one mode will support development in the others.

For these children in particular certain aspects of classroom planning can be most helpful in easing the child's entry into a strange and potentially stressful situation:

(1) Before the pupil joins the class it is important for the class teacher to have as much information about the newcomer as possible.

If time allows, a display of appropriate books in dual or original text in the child's first language might be made, along with suitable tapes or pictures. Labelling and focussing on different scripts throughout the school will demostrate to the children and their families that home languages are valued. Every effort should be made to translate school communication to parents if this is necessary.

(2) Arrange for other pupils to look after the new pupil. One of these might be a child who shares the same first language, if this is a possibility. The establishing of supportive partners right from the start can be most valuable in the building up of friendships.

(3) Seat newcomers so that they can be involved with other pupils and where they can actively participate with group work wherever possible. (Games involving repetitive language can be

very helpful here.) Activities in which meanings are made clear through the actions of others in the group are ideal, as is the support for children's understanding offered by pictures and real objects.

(4) Remember that it is very tiring to listen to a new language for long periods and children may want to play quietly in the home corner for parts of the day, or may enjoy listening to home language tapes in the 'listening corner'.

(5) Be ready to provide extra loving care and patience which may be essential if you are to gain the confidence of a child who cannot yet speak English. A few phrases learnt in their home language could provide comfort and help you to build a relationship with your new pupil.

Classroom opportunities

Pat Jones (1988) refers to a 'climate for talk' (p. 164) and the importance of creating a warm and conducive environment in the school. It would seem then that after initial considerations for a new child's well-being, the organisation and lay-out of the classroom should be a major concern. The teacher no doubt will be aiming to provide her bilingual pupils with opportunities to talk and listen in a variety of contexts. Any area of the classroom or piece of equipment can provide worthwhile settings, be it the sink or the painting easels. Working in pairs or small groups, however, will encourage conversation in less confident speakers, especially if the room is arranged in a way that makes this possible. Although it is obviously a great deal easier to organize the working space when furniture is multi-purpose and adaptable, even more important will be the feeling amongst children that they are free to adapt and find the most appropriate setting for an activity. Drawing the line between a lively classroom where children are actively learning through talk, and an environment where it is so noisy that a timid child finds it difficult to compete, can be hard. However, with help even young children can come to understand that talking and listening are a part of their 'real work'. They may then appreciate that sharing ideas, finding solutions and learning through interaction will require a collaborative rather than competitive atmosphere in the classroom, and consideration for one another.

In addition to sections for small group work every classroom needs an area where the class can assemble to share their experiences. For bilingual children plenty of listening time is important and teachers should not be concerned if new pupils are initially reluctant to contribute orally. Whole class experiences will be supporting oral language development in a variety of ways and through a wide range of activities, whether it is by sharing with the class something they have made in a group session, or listening to stories and poems.

Space permitting there is also a need for more private areas where children can meet and play, away from immediate adult attention and intervention. The 'home corner' in whatever guise, for example a 'doctor's waiting room', 'hairdressers' or 'post office', is an invaluable resource for the young bilingual child. This is partly for the opportunities such a setting may offer to bridge the gap between home and school experiences. A selection of dressing up clothes reflecting the cultural groups in the classroom (Aunins, 1990) for example, could offer endless opportunities for discussion.

A 'Listening Area' can be set up to include a range of materials suitable for a bilingual child. Taped stories, for example, can be made by the children and adults and these can be usefully accompanied by books, models and cut-out figures which do much to support a child's understanding as they listen. The tapes can of course be in the languages spoken by bilingual pupils as well as in English. It can be especially useful for children to share their listening experiences with a friend.

The physical setting of the classroom will be a key factor in the class teacher's planning and may give rise to experimenting as she explores different ways of developing the linguistic resources her pupils have. She may well find it helpful to share some of these thoughts, problems and ideas with other colleagues and this might be a most valuable first step in formulating whole school policies on language diversity.

The following is a collection of strategies that have been found useful and might provide starting points for teachers to use in their own individual contexts.

Finding out about language diversity

Many teachers have found a real value in giving increased recognition to their pupils' home languages. Indeed, in working with bilingual pupils this would seem to be of paramount importance, for the way that we speak can be seen as a cornerstone of our identity. Investigations of language and dialect are therefore relevant and of value to the whole class. The National Curriculum makes specific reference to the positive asset bilingual pupils bring in increasing their classmates' knowledge about the nature of language. Investigations carried out in early years classrooms are likely to be informal in nature, and may be greatly enhanced through discussions with families and other community members. Close consultation with parents is important, not only for the valuable help they can give, but also so that they can understand the school's interest in their mother tongue and its importance in the child's gradual mastery of English.

Gathering information by the children about the languages of their school or classroom can easily be developed into cross curricular activities. Their findings for example, collected perhaps through a simple questionnaire, could be presented in graph form and much rich discussion might ensue. Looking at the names of the children in the class and finding out their meanings might be another fruitful starting point, and might develop into an investigation of the different naming traditions in various cultures.

Displays around the classroom of different scripts and languages may include, for example, other number systems, alphabets and the names of colours. Children are often fascinated by such charts and ensuing discussions may have the added value of placing bilingual pupils in the role of 'expert' as they share their greater knowledge with the class. Labels around the classroom reflecting the children's first languages can do much to help a bilingual pupil feel that the classroom atmosphere is hospitable to diversity and such a positive atmosphere will reap educational benefits for bilingual pupils and indeed for the class as a whole.

Across the curriculum

It is useful for teachers planning topic work for their class to build in a multilingual element wherever this is possible. Many of the recurring school themes such as 'seasons' and 'festivals' can lead to a wide range of language-stimulating activities. One teacher's diary of a term's work on 'Harvest' for example, describes how her top infant classroom became a hive of activity. Class discussion, group planning, individual and paired research, followed by feedback to the class and reporting to the teacher all involved her bilingual pupils in very useful ways. Links between home and school were strengthened as children brought in labels from food as a starting point for finding out about harvests from different countries. Parents became involved in the cooking of dishes of different cultural origins and the children were able to visit local markets in small groups and to bring back and share their experiences with the rest of the class. One such visit proved to be a real turning point for a small, rather withdrawn Chinese girl. For the preparation in the classroom of a dish of noodles by Yasmin and her mother was a tumultuous success as the class teacher's diary reports:

> Yasmin had a wonderful afternoon! She explained how the vegetables had to be prepared for the dish and organised the children as helpers in a delightful way.

In this way a valuable link was made between Yasmin's home and school worlds, as well as giving her a new role as an 'expert'. The class book made with the photographs of Yasmin's cooking demonstration and completed with a text in Chinese and English became her favourite reading material for a long while to come.

Cookery can give rise to just the kind of informal setting which can be of such benefit to a bilingual child. Activities which encourage the attention of an adult who has the time to explore and perhaps extend the child's meanings in a non-threatening way are invaluable. One school developed a theme on 'crops' to include experiments with different types of flour and made breads of different cultural origins. This short taped transcript came from one of these activities:

> Adult: That's lovely isn't it? What should we do with the rolls now?
> Mark: Put the dish in here Ripa ... in here carefully.
> Ripa: One, two, three ... more.
> Mark: Yes I know you're getting more rolls ... that's because ...
> Adult: Are you counting them Ripa?
> Ripa: My Mummy, my Daddy, My Tarik ...
> Mark: Oh yes! You'll need one for all the people in your family.

Ripa's English is still limited and yet in the context of what she was doing she was successfuly able to convey her meanings to Mark. He in turn demonstrates the powerful role that a bilingual child's peers can play in developing their oral language.

Why story?

The vital importance of storying to a young child is discussed fully in another chapter of this book. Suffice then to say that stories in their widest context are one of the most valuable sources for any class teacher whose aim is to develop her bilingual pupils' speaking and listening skills. For stories provide a simple means of bringing the language and experiences of the wider world into the classroom and have the potential of giving vivid insights into other cultures and backgrounds. They may also provide deeply satisfying enjoyment for the children and an experience to be shared with others.

Children are helped to make sense of their own lives through listening to the tales of others and this may well encourage bilingual pupils to share their experiences and to contribute their own stories and accounts. For there is little doubt that stories can provide a tremendous stimulus for spoken language when pupils are encouraged to retell them in their own words and, of course, home languages. Stories also provide an ideal starting point for work across the curriculum, and may introduce children to new and relevant language in the context of what they are studying. Finally, in what better way could a young bilingual child develop the vital story telling skills that they will use all their lives, than by taking part in a variety of such activities first hand? For as they become aware of the 'patterns' within stories and the needs of their audience they will begin to develop into skilful story tellers themselves. Amongst the National Oracy Project's excellent publications there are several which develop this theme, including a delightful booklet entitled: *Gathering and Presenting Evidence/Telling Stories in School* (N.O.P. 1988).

Conclusion: Some ways of encouraging talk in bilingual pupils

- Aim to provide as many first hand experiences as possible. Bilingual children have much to gain from working collaboratively in the classroom, as English is drawn from and related to the curriculum activities and learning contexts of the classroom.
- Give plenty of opportunities for revisiting activities and for re-listening, rehearsing and revising.
- Remember that any learning situation can be adapted to develop a child's oral language.
- Bilingual children need models for learning the English language. Teachers should aim at providing a wide range of models within the classroom. These can be their peers, older pupils in the school and, of course, other adults.
- Good home-school links will be very important for the English

language development of bilingual pupils. Great care must therefore be taken to explain to families the school's policies and to convey the concern for bilingualism within the school. It is essential that schools and teachers make their approaches to teaching explicit, in order that families and schools can work together in supporting the child.

CHAPTER 5

The Language Needs of the Young Traveller Child

Fran Duncan

'We're playing scrapyards', was the reply to my question. It was obvious of course, or should have been. Visiting a Travelling family who were temporarily residing on a scrapyard where they worked, I encountered three small children kneeling in front of an old sofa outside their trailer. On the sofa were several neat piles of metals, carefully being sorted into copper, tin, steel and iron. Children who live in a house will play 'houses', so why not 'scrapyards' in a scrapyard? Looking more closely, I saw just how accurately and carefully the children were sorting the metals. They could also tell me how much by weight each metal would be worth. These children were five and six years old.

All children come into school with a unique personal culture, whatever their ethnic origin. As educators we need to affirm and respect what each child brings. When referring to the 'Travelling Community' it is important to be aware that we are not looking at a homogenous group, any more than within the 'housed' community. What all 'Travellers' do have in common is the fact that their homes are mobile. Within this mobile community are groups as diverse as Showpeople, Circus Travellers, Bargees, Gypsy Travellers and New Age Travellers, all with very different roots. For all Travelling children, however, their security lies in the home and family. Where the family is, the home is. Place, in the sense of geographical location, is of little importance compared with people. It is vital for us to understand this and not to perceive mobility as a negative aspect of the Travelling child's experience. It may make it more difficult for us to ensure full access to the school curriculum, but that is our problem, not theirs. We must find ways of fitting our delivery to the lifestyle rather than attempting to enforce the reverse.

It is not feasible in one chapter to consider the needs of every group of children within the Travelling Community; that would need a book in itself. I intend, therefore, to concentrate specifically on the Gypsy Travellers, with the premise that many of the needs considered will also have implications for the wider group. It is important to look in some detail at the ancestry of the European Gypsies to set the context. We need to understand the discrimination and persecutions these people have experienced in order to fully appreciate the needs of their children. This also helps the children realise that they too *have* a history, they have roots; as well as helping teachers to value the children.

The term 'Gypsy' comes from 'Little Egypt', a part of Northern India where the Gypsy Travellers originated. European Gypsies left there about 1,000 years ago, travelling in small family groups seeking work such as blacksmithing, metal working, horse dealing, shoe making, and various forms of entertainment. There have been many theories about the ethnic origins of Gypsy people but according to various sources, one being Liegeois (1986), 'it finally became possible to locate the country of origin of this Romani language: India'.

From the outset, the Gypsies were regarded with mistrust and suspicion wherever they arrived; partly because of their dark skin, use of their own language and their apparent lack of roots and belonging in any place. At that time, and indeed until recently according to Kenrick and Puxon (1972), Romani was the only Indian language spoken in Europe. They quote the remarks of a Spaniard:

> When I go to market, there in the corner stand the accursed Gypsies, jabbering to each other in a speech which I cannot understand.

In many countries, gypsies who did wish to attend religious observances had to listen through the window outside the churches. The Church in Western Europe rejected them. In 1560, a Swedish Archbishop declared, 'The Priest shall not concern himself with Gypsies; He shall neither bury their corpses, nor christen their children' (Kenrick and Puxon, 1972). They also experienced exclusion because of their practice of telling fortunes.

The Church was joined by the two other pillars of power in Medieval Europe, the State and the Trade Guilds, in its marginalisation of the Gypsy people. Throughout the continent a policy of expulsion was adopted; punishments for not complying were horrendous. In many countries, 'Gypsy-Hunting' became a sport and these were hunts to kill. In Prague in 1710 an edict was issued stating that all adult men should be hanged without trial and women and children mutilated, presumably so they could not reproduce.

In Germany the hatred of Gypsies climaxed in the gas chambers. Estimates of the number of Gypsies exterminated vary from 300,000 to 500,000. A detailed account of this tragic episode in Gypsy history can be found in Kenrick and Puxon (1972). It was also shown on the B.B.C. Television Production, televised in 1989, 'Forgotten Holocaust'. A recent poem by a Gypsy, Charlie Smith, provides an epitaph for these people:

> Where are the monuments
> Where are the stones
> They're nowhere to be seen
> for all the Gypsy people murdered
> by the Nazi Regime. (Charlie Smith, 1990)

Smith states in his Foreword:

> When I am asked if I am a 'Real Gypsy', my answer is this: 'I am flesh and blood, I feel pain, I feel joy, I love, I hate, cut me I bleed, I am a real human being living in today's world who happens to be a Gypsy. Not some Stereotype that fits misinformed people's ideas of what a Gypsy should be'.

Discrimination continues even in Britain today. In 1959 Gypsies were prohibited from camping in a highway (Section 127 of the Highways Act), although non-Gypsies remained free to do so. The 1968 Caravan Sites Act requires local authorities to 'provide adequate accommodation for Gypsies residing in or resorting to their area.' In exchange for this obligation, they have the right to prohibit camping in other places and to remove offenders.

It is estimated that Local Authorities have spent more money on digging trenches, erecting barricades and evicting Travellers, than on providing 'suitable accommodation'.

> Our new town's alright with its shiny new homes,
> Of new red brick and chrome
> But some Travelling people pulled up last week
> And they live in a mobile home
> But we soon shifted them with the council van,
> We'll give no peace to a Travelling Man. (Nathan Lee, 1978)

I know of Travellers being evicted at 2 a.m., small children roused from their sleep, trailers hitched to lorries and pulled over county boundaries. Some counties deny having a 'Traveller problem' by ensuring that evictions take place just before the official annual trailer count, thus exempting themselves from any responsibility for site provision. Annex 2 of D.O.E. Circular 8/81, which sets out criteria for designation, states: 'authorities should undertake to use enforcement powers with compassion'! Liegeois writes, 'At bottom, the way Gypsies are treated has less to do with laws than with the state of mind shaped by myths and stereotypes'.

Prior to the early 1970's, very little was done in Britain to take education to the Travellers and the idea of informing the settled community about Travellers is an even more recent development. Although no exact figures are available, it is estimated that at the present time 80% of Primary aged Travelling children and 20% of Secondary age are receiving schooling.

The watershed for Traveller Education came in 1967, when Lady Plowden described Travelling children as Britain's most educationally deprived group. Gradually Local Authorities, with the help of a Government grant, began to meet their responsibilities to the Travelling community by appointing teachers as outreach workers to build a bridge between the Travellers and the Education System. There are still, however, authorities who are not fulfilling this obligation.

In the case of many young children of ethnic minority origin within our schools we may be in the situation where we do not understand their language. With the Traveller Gypsy child, we are looking more at dialect and word usage. When the Romani peoples left India they took with them their language. Travelling through Persia and into Europe, this became syntactically adapted to that of the host country, retaining the original lexical content. The Romani spoken by today's English Travellers is a dialect of English with the Romani words inserted into English syntax.

Where a gorgio (non-Gypsy) is present family members may converse in Romani English if they wish to communicate privately. Acton and Kenrick (1984) observe that when meeting a stranger, a Traveller Gypsy may speak Romani to identify the ethnicity of that person. Alternatively, knowing that a sympathetic gorgio will usually understand some Romani words, it can be a way of checking a person out before asking for help or advice. The similarity, however, with the Indian language spoken by the original Gypsies remains, as is illustrated by a story told by a Travelling friend. A group of local Travelling women visited an Indian restaurant for an evening meal. During the meal some of the Indian waiters began conversing in

Punjabi in not very complimentary terms about their clientele. Imagine their embarrassment when one of the women replied in Romani, having understood their remarks.

The Romani language, or dialect, has been passed down orally, although it is presently being documented. If teachers are aware of a child's early vocabulary in terms of feelings and namings, this will obviously enable more effective communication when the young child arrives in nursery or school. The following is a list, compiled from my own experience, of words most commonly encountered amongst the Gypsy Travellers.

PEOPLE		NAMING ANIMALS/OBJECTS	
babby	– baby	trailer	– caravan
gorgio ⎫ gaujo ⎭	– non-Traveller	motor	– car
		waggon	– lorry
muskerers	– police	hotchi-witchi	– hedgehog
chavvies	– children	kongeri	– church
chai	– girl	roolie	– waggon
chavvi	– boy	vardo	– living waggon
didikai	– half-gypsy	gissie	– pig
dukkerer	– fortune teller	long-boy	– rat
mush	– man		

FEELINGS

kushti	– good; kushti-bok – good luck
rajjed	– stirred up inside
ladged	– ashamed
divvi	– mad, daft
trashed	– frightened

The purpose of outlining the cultural origins and language roots of the Gypsy Travellers and the close knit family structures common to all Travellers is to emphasise that those concerned with the education of Traveller children should begin by acknowledging that, 'theirs is a culture having as much integrity as our own'. (Acton and Kenrick, 1984). We have already established that the majority of young Travelling children will come into school from a closely knit family background where they are well cared for and protected. Most of their social interaction will have been with the adults and children within their own extended family group. Travelling children are rarely 'talked down' to and baby language is virtually unknown. Consequently, even the very young child will often have a maturity of oral language, although they may be initially reticent about communicating with people they do not know.

A colleague told me of her experience while visiting the home of a local Travelling family. Kenny, a boy aged three, patted his knee while saying to his two year old sister, 'Come on, my babby, come and sit on my knee'. He also goes out with his father to the scrapyard and was heard to say, as he gave his sister money from his earnings, 'Don't tell mammy'. Remember the three children 'playing scrap-yards' at the beginning? All of these children are learning, at a very early age, their role in life. Is this unusual? I think not. Children play will dolls, travel in cars, follow their parents around 'helping' in every walk of life. The difference lies in the particular skills being acquired.

Amongst Travelling people, sex roles are usually clearly defined. While boys are learning about scrap metal, for example, girls will be helping to look after their younger siblings or cleaning inside the trailers, which are immaculate. There is potential here for possible cultural misunderstanding in the teacher/child relationship, although this applies to many groups in society, not just the Travelling Community where male/female roles are very clearly defined. Having said this, it is not appropriate to over-generalise. For example, I found when visiting a family that all six children aged between four and seventeen were helping to make the beautiful dolls which are sold at various Fairs in the North of England. While one person sews, another will wind lace, another dress the dolls, another pack the finished dolls into boxes (as Jo said, 'what they don't use from ASDA'). While the family work together, their mother is talking, telling stories about her past life. Once at the Fairs, everyone, apart from the very youngest, will help with the selling. A wonderful example of a self-sufficient family cooperative.

The story-telling tradition is an important element of Traveller culture. Duncan Williamson has written down collections of stories he was told as a child, from his grandmother's 'pocket' (a kind of purse). The family travelled in traditional bender tents and evening entertainment was to settle around the fire and listen to stories, stories which were designed to teach the young Travelling children codes of conduct for later life, as with Traditional tales from every culture. Personal experience would suggest, however, that most oral tradition amongst Travellers is historical rather than fictional.

I have spent many hours listening to older Travellers talking about their life 'on the road'. Sadly, they are no longer as mobile and much of their freedom to travel has been eroded. From an early age

Travelling children are told stories relating to their past and quickly develop a feeling for their own roots and culture. They will come into school with a very definite sense of identity, which must be accepted and affirmed for home/school 'bonding' to be established.

It is important not to fall into the trap of stereotyping, as Travelling people, like any other group in society, cannot be encapsulated in a few statements. However, generally speaking, most Travelling children will bring into school: strong family bonding; confidence with adults, yet a possible diffidence with strangers; a strong sense of identity; an early sense of future role in life.

Bernstein's view cannot be too strongly emphasised: If the culture of the teacher is to become part of the consciousness of the child, then the culture of the child must be in the consciousness of the teacher. This may mean that the teacher must first be able to understand the child's dialect rather than deliberately attempt to change it. (Bernstein, 1974).

To implement this advice in relation to the young Traveller child entering the gorgio education system, Acton and Kenrick state, 'teachers must be aware of the inter-action of culture and language in the Travellers' use of English'.

> *Metz Bridge – Middlesbrough*
> 'This is a *car*, Harold.
> It's a *motor*, miss.
> This is a *lorry*, Harold.
> It's a *truck*, miss.
> This is a *house*, Harold.
> I'm not a *housey*, miss.
> You are a *traveller*, Harold.
> I'm a *gypsy*, miss.
> This is a *caravan*, Harold.
> It's a *trailer*, miss,
> and it's chained to the ground'. (Molly Maughan, 1984)

This again emphasises the need for the teacher to be aware not only of words which are specifically of Romani origin, but also different usage of English vocabulary.

How can we as educators build on the positive experiences a young Travelling child brings into the school situation, without making that child feel 'different'?

We need to create a welcoming environment, culturally appropriate to all children. This could be complicated if we are in a multi-ethnic school, where we have several groups represented. Take the home corner for example. Can we represent the home of a Travelling child, a child of Chinese origin, a child of Asian origin, or do we create a mainstream white environment because our culture dictates this is the appropriate role model?

Are there books and pictures in school to which all children can relate? Do we talk about 'Homes' as synonymous with 'Houses'? Do we treat children from a minority group as an oddity? Or is our environment such that everyone's culture is represented, with all children having equal access to what is provided? One young boy of eight said to me, 'I don't want to go to a new school. They'll do "Circuses" again.' He is from a Circus family and this was the school's approach to welcoming him. The intentions were good, but the child's reaction speaks volumes.

Paulo Freire in his *Education as the Price of Freedom* (1967), was actually expounding his educational method for teaching illiterate adults. His premise was that the educator should start where the person is, developing initial social sight vocabulary from his own background. When we introduce children to their first sight vocabulary, what are the images we use? Following Freire's model, the Travelling child would be introduced to 'trailer', 'motor', 'horse', 'dog' and so forth. There is much to commend the use of photographs and children's drawings when compiling early reading materials. Desk-top publishing can lead to 'professional' reading books which can be shared with other children. Even very young children can produce words and drawings around the theme 'the way I live'. In the multi-cultural classroom this can lead to a rich sharing and affirmation of one another's personal cultures.

A colleague from our Service in Cleveland was working with an ethnically mixed group of children which included Travellers, on the theme just mentioned, 'The way I live'. Rosie's book wonderfully encapsulates her own personal culture. While her housed friends have described their houses, she begins, 'Here is my new trailer' and takes us on a guided tour in pictures. She illustrates the family pets, 'This is John's horse'. 'This is Davey's dog'. Not, 'This is our dog', as may be more usual in mainstream culture. She describes Appleby as her 'best site' because, 'I meet my cousins'. Fairs are where Travelling folk meet and catch up with each other. It's there, in her book. She tells us, 'My dad deals with the men and my mam cleans up', illustrated by dad and 'Willie' shaking hands as they do a deal. She writes about constant evictions, 'Everywhere we pull the councils come and they say you'll have to pull off... You have to pack down because they shift us'.

Figure 1   My best site.
My best site is at Appleby. There is lots of trailers and lots of people. I meet my cousins.

Figure 2   They complain if you don't sweep your slab.

The attitudes of authority towards herself and family come out in phrases such as, 'the warden is always shouting' and, 'They complain if you don't sweep your slab' . . . 'They're always complaining about something. They complain about dogs. They complain about my dad's horse and it's in the field and my dad argues'.

She describes her experience in her least favourite school, 'I never had nowt to do – they used to leave you with nothing to do and they never helped you when you needed help'.

There are many messages here for us to heed as teachers and authority figures, ('they').

Another example of good practice in encouraging all children to share their experience is that of another teacher working in a multi-ethnic school which included Travelling children. She had a table set aside where children could place anything they wished from home.

At a time of their own choosing, the children could share with the group and talk about what they had brought in an informal session. In the group was Jake, a young Travelling lad of about seven, who

Figure 3   My Dad deals with the men and my Mam cleans up. Big boys and little boys throw mud balls.

had not been very communicative. One day he came into school carrying a tin can, a knife and some strips of wood which he placed on the table. His teacher was not very happy about the penknife, but explained to the children that while they could touch the other objects, they should not touch that, keeping a very close eye on it. The next day, Jake indicated he would like to talk to the other children. He proceeded to make clothes pegs, explaining the process to his fascinated classmates. The following day several children appeared complete with tin cans, wood and penknives, asking Jake's help in manufacturing their own clothes pegs. The enterprising lad not only helped them make their pegs. At the end of the session, having already explained he made them to sell, he collected them all in and took home!

A group of children in one of our infant schools was given the game 'make a house' to work with. One of the Travelling children said, 'I don't want to make a house', to which her support teacher replied, 'Make a trailer then'. Rosie and Jacob proceeded to invent their own version of the game, making cardboard trailers, water-churns, tow bars, doors and windows and a colour coded dice. That particular teacher had the insight to allow these children to embark on a constructive, culturally appropriate activity as a spontaneous part of what was happening in the classroom. Other children were, of course, allowed 'a turn' of Rosie and Jacob's game – all part of sharing one another's culture.

How can we help the ethnic minority children in our care to bridge the cultural gap, while valuing the heritage they bring from home? I have begun to make some suggestions by giving examples of good practice which I hope will be helpful. But this is only a starting point. Paulo Freire has the philosophy that rather than attempting to 'socialise' minority groups into the 'power' (or mainstream) society, we should enrich and help these groups to feel emancipated and strong in their own right, strong enough to challenge authority. We need to ask ourselves if our aim in teaching children is to assimilate them into the 'power' society, or to help them gain enough strength and self esteem to retain their identity as equals, yet different. Helping children in the acquisition of language skills, be it oral communication, reading or writing, is one way we can give them choices and help them decode the world around them. The needs of the young Traveller child are not simply to read and write and retain a sense of culture, but to continue that culture into future generations from a position of greater strength. Perhaps I should simply say 'from a position of equality'.

CHAPTER 6

Building on Bilingualism: Issues of Access and Assessment in the Curriculum

Judith Lawton

Because bilingual children come to school able to speak languages other than English, they start with the possibility of quickly developing extra language skills if they are given the proper support. We must take advantage of this learning potential and build upon their bilingualism. Being bilingual can be an incentive to exploring, comparing, enquiring and learning, rather than a drawback, especially when valued and built upon. Bilingual pupils in the classroom also provide greater opportunities for teachers to develop language awareness for all pupils.

An example of drawing on the pre-school experiences of children of different backgrounds is provided in 'Education for Citizenship' (NCC, 1990):

> Pupils listen to a story (e.g. *The Tiger Who Came to Tea* by J. Kerr) as a starting point for their thematic work. Pupils discuss different roles in the family and other groups, learn about other countries, languages and ways of life, try different kinds of food and ways of cooking . . . .
> (Appendix 2, p. 20)

A related use of this same book occurred when one Language teacher worked with bilingual parents to make some dual language text books and tape recordings in Vietnamese and Korean. This was in a Nursery school where only two boys could speak these languages. They also made a large book to share, magnet board pictures, and a picture lotto game based on the story, while the children themselves helped to make a book, with other nursery children, of their own pretend tea-making. The involvement of these children in interactive listening and speaking activities inevitably served to support their language development.

Thus, as this example shows, the presence of developing bilingual pupils can encourage a stimulating curriculum planned to embrace perspectives from a variety of cultures and traditions, which will inevitably benefit everyone. In acknowledging linguistic diversity in the classroom as an asset, the National Curriculum Council say:

> It provides an opportunity for pupils to gain first hand experience, knowledge and understanding of other cultures and perspectives. It also helps to prepare pupils for life in a multicultural society by promoting respect for all forms of language. (Circular 11, 1991)

Language skills gained while acquiring a first language are transferable skills. Children who can understand and speak a Home language, and who recognise that written symbols in that language represent sounds or words, will begin to assimilate the new sounds and signs of the English in the classroom. They will make connections with what they already know, especially when encouraged to do so in a classroom labelled in various languages.

For a policy which takes into account, and develops to the full, the learning potential of second language children, it is vital to forge the positive links between:

- Expectation and achievement
- Provision and performance
- Access and assessment.

High expectation linked with high achievement

Teacher expectation can be reinforced:

- by acknowledging that knowing more than one language benefits educational progress generally;
- by remembering that research confirms that general language development is underpinned by bilingualism;
- by full involvement of bilingual pupils in this expectation of ultimate high achievement.

This shared expectation should result in strong motivation for both pupils and teachers to demand of each other a commitment to finding ways to build upon this bilingualism.

Appropriate provision linked with enhanced performance

Provision needs to be supported by the awareness that the Nursery or classroom should be enriched by our many cultured society and, if possible, reflect the cultural backgrounds of all the children. A supportive and anti-racist learning situation will enable bilingual children to take risks in learning and perform at their best without fear of censure or ridicule.

In addition, provision of practical learning activities across the curriculum, with opportunities for interactive group work, will motivate all young learners and offer developing bilingual pupils both immediate involvement and the means and incentive to communicate. Language teachers, where available, will provide purpose-made materials and strategies to facilitate this, in addition to clearly focused English language extension.

Where bilingual pupils lack this additional specialist support, class teachers, coping alone, may make good use of published materials, such as the Hounslow Language Service Primary Team's *Fruit Project Pack*. Packs of this kind provide a much-needed wealth of materials for ready planned learning activities.

A key factor in implementing all these aspects of appropriate provision must be adequate Teacher Resources, including a good pupil–teacher ratio and sufficient additional language teachers.

Full access and fair assessment

For the bilingual learner, full access to the curriculum is a vital prerequisite for fair assessment of progress within it. The ongoing assessment of growing strengths, developing language skills and learning needs indicates which supportive measures will contribute to greater curriculum access. This in turn will help children to develop at an appropriate conceptual level. Supportive measures may be as simple as allowing additional time for the completion of a task or ensuring that instructions for a learning or assessment activity are clearly understood. Instructions may be clarified by devices such as:

- interpreting in mother-tongue;
- demonstrating the task;
- using a diagram;
- drawing a series of simple pictures;
- providing a simplified version;

- arranging for another pupil to guide them through an activity step by step;
- using gesture, facial expressions, body language;
- ensuring initially that the language of instruction is consistent over a range of tasks;
- displaying a series of one word prompts, ideally in both English and the relevant home languages, e.g. in the painting area a poster might be provided (see Figure 1).

Figure 1

Remember:

apron

Name

picture

wash

Full access to the whole curriculum is the statutory right of every pupil. This may be facilitated by using assessment procedures in order to identify children's language skills and language support needs, as a preliminary to planning teaching provision, with the guidance of Language Support teachers, where available. Teacher assessment of bilingual pupils' language development needs is a continuous process, informing and modifying schemes of work and learning activities as they are planned, reviewed and evaluated. For all pupils, assessment needs to be based partly on observation of the children's classroom responses, behaviour and contribution to group work and partly on evidence of individual achievement and progress.

To underpin the high expectation and achievement, optimum provision and performance, and full access, a range of appropriate procedures has been devised. These are designed and used by language teachers in different local areas. What they have in common, whatever their format, is that they are formulated to identify and/or record not only what bilingual children need to learn, but also their written and spoken language attainments, in English and in their first language, if possible.

For each child starting nursery or infant school, schools generally draw up an Initial Pupil Profile, recording name, age, and similar details. In order to make the best use of the initial meeting with a parent, and to ensure that home/school links are established from the beginning, many schools have wisely added sections to record information about the child's main Home language, the language skills of the parent, the ethnic background, the religion and any dietary requirements. All this can help the school understand the cultural context for the child's early concept development. *Language Profiles* for young bilingual pupils should record fuller detail, such as the language or languages spoken or heard in use, any known literacy skills in one of the home languages, any mother tongue classes attended or awards gained outside school, and any other known achievements. Early assessments should record aptitudes which can be encouraged in language learning, such as:

- the ability to repeat new vocabulary fairly accurately;
- the ability to learn new vocabulary when taught;
- an eagerness to communicate;
- indications of understanding more than can yet be communicated orally.

To enable teachers to record later progress in English, any evidence of current awareness should be noted – for instance, any English words understood or spoken, and any letters of the English alphabet they can recognise. This initial assessment elicits non-verbal and then verbal responses by using as a stimulus materials readily found in the Infant school, such as coloured shapes, model furniture, animals or cars, or a doll family, if possible of the child's own ethnic origin. To make the child feel at ease, the context should be warm, comfortable, quiet, and if possible familiar. If the assessment has to take place in the classroom, there should, at least, be pictures and objects relevant to the child's culture present. The child's responses should be recorded unobtrusively, and pauses for thought allowed. The teacher should arrange a chance to play or chat informally with the child before and after the language assessment procedure, and may find it useful to provide a prepared check sheet. Materials should be devised to engage the interest of the child and stimulate a variety of responses – for instance: gesture (pointing to an object); action, such as placing a baby cow near a mummy cow; one word answers, such as 'yes' or 'there'; fuller answers, to both open and closed questions, and unprompted responses. A tape recorder, preferably hidden, so that longer utterances can be analysed later, is also valuable.

A teacher-made *Second Stage Assessment* procedure can provide opportunities for assessment of a further range of language skills. The child listens to a story of a suitable level being read, then answers prepared questions on it, does a sequencing activity and perhaps some related writing. Skills thus assessed might include listening comprehension, use of more complex language structures and functions, and sequencing and predicting.

As children progress, a *Yearly Language Record* can also indicate, in summary, the teacher's assessment of levels in English in relation to the National Curriculum Attainment Targets. In order to focus upon some specific lexis or language structure, a teacher may preselect an activity which will generate the desired language use. The advantage of this kind of procedure is that the child is at ease and responding naturally, using language in the classroom context and interacting with the peer group. Specific prompts on an observational check list might include: 'sings a song or rhyme in a group'; 'talks to other children'.

Armed with knowledge gained from appropriate assessment and records of progress, teachers will be in a position to draw upon resource materials and to select strategies which will help make the curriculum accessible. They should also manage the classroom in order to make the learning situation comfortable, welcoming, non-threatening, anti-racist and multicultural. A supportive environment for this process would, ideally, include bilingual teaching support in the child's home language, though this may not always be practicable, given that about two hundred different languages may be used in British classrooms. In addition, group and pair work with pupils more fluent in English, particularly with those who share the same Mother tongue, has also proved to be valuable.

Bilingual pupils and special educational needs provision

Children developing bilingualism should always be given time and encouragement to listen and to observe without a response being expected. It has been shown that there may be a silent listening period when children first find themselves in a classroom where English is the teaching medium, before they can bring themselves to speak. It is important that pupils at this 'silent stage' should not be mistakenly identified as slow learners, and withdrawn for Special Needs support. It should be remembered that while a few bilingual children do have special educational needs, being bilingual is not, in itself, a cause for concern, but rather a cause for celebration. In order to develop concepts vital for their education, children need, for the most part, to be in the classroom and to benefit from all the learning experiences and activities available there.

However, with greater emphasis on summative achievement and recording of results for Infant school children, there is some concern that children learning and being tested in their second language will appear to be low achievers, something which would worsen their self-esteem and reinforce the myth about bilingual under-achievement. As well as the possible distress caused to pupils, this can have the effect of causing low teacher expectation.

It is, however, clear that some bilingual pupils *will* have special needs, and the problem of assessing these is inevitably more difficult than that for first language speakers. Amongst the most telling aspects are:

- any known medical or psychological factors
- any marked discrepancy between the child's progress in school and that of her or his peer group.

Checklists to assist this rather specialised assessment and identification of needs have been drawn up, but where a class teacher teaches with Language Support teachers or Special Educational Needs Support teachers, the knowledge which these specialists have of the relevant criteria may be sought. Where there is access to a teacher or other suitable adult with the same mother-tongue, the pupil's mother-tongue ability may be considered, which is a useful indicator of progress to be expected in English. A support visit undertaken by such a teacher provides a chance for an informal meeting of pupil, parents and class teachers, which is frequently mutually helpful.

Although any 'Bilingual assessment' in these circumstances cannot be official, additional insights about the pupil help the teacher to differentiate the curriculum. As well as covering the kind of knowledge about the child which has already been discussed above, such as the linguistic and cultural background, this kind of procedure can enable the teacher:

- to liaise with parents and show that their additional language skills are valued;
- to identify which language skills in English need specific support and to select the most appropriate form of support for a pupil experiencing pronounced learning difficulties;
- to observe bilingual children working in the classroom and to contribute notes from the observation to inform shared teacher planning.

In every case the purpose of the procedure is to provide a clear idea of the bilingual children's particular strengths or their learning needs, so making a positive educational contribution. The usefulness and effectiveness of some procedures, although diagnostic in purpose, depend to a great degree on teachers' experience and awareness of other factors which can affect the performance of bilingual children. For example, care must be exercised with Screening Procedures. These are followed at five and seven in some Local Education Authorities to try to establish which children may be experiencing difficulties, for example, in emotional stability. They rely upon teachers being able to identify types of behaviour that give cause for concern. It should be remembered that some responses or even lack of response may be related to a child's experience as a second language learner. For example, children described as 'tense', 'anxious', 'withdrawn' or 'aggressive' and thus identified as 'giving cause for concern' may be reacting to factors such as lack of fluency in English, the shock of transition from one culture to another, or not being used to the English school system. If so, rather than labelling the child as 'emotionally unstable', we can take action to remedy or ease the difficulties causing the adverse reactions.

Bilingual pupils and the National Curriculum

Teachers need to be aware of some possible dangers for bilingual pupils in relation to National Curriculum assessment and access. Bilingualism in itself is not a reason for disapplication from the statutory assessment procedures. Disapplication, with its attendant reduction of access to the whole curriculum on the grounds of insufficient English, has to be accompanied by a planned programme to remedy what is seen as a deficit. This procedure is based on the false assumption that a bilingual beginner should be taken aside to have some English language skills instilled before facing the difficult and demanding curriculum work. We know however that the bilingual child learning English needs:

- chances to hear English used in the learning context by peer group language models;
- opportunities to practise the new language in real situations;
- involvement in activities that stimulate relevant talk;
- time to listen, observe and acquire English;
- support from more fluent speakers of English;
- chances, where someone else shares the home language, to switch from language to language;
- the learning environment of a supportive classroom.

There is a temptation to disapply bilingual pupils who may be expected to achieve low scores in the Standard Assessment Tasks (SATs), particularly when decision making is influenced by awareness of issues like publication of results, parental choice, open enrolment, and opting out.

When bilingual children are included in the statutory assessment procedures, both the curriculum related Teacher Assessment and the SATs, extra care must be taken to guard against the influence of low teacher expectation. In addition, teachers should find supportive strategies and familiar material that enable the children to demonstrate their knowledge and grasp of concepts.

A variety of ways in which children in the early stages of English Language development may demonstrate their knowledge and understanding should be explored. Instead of verbal or written responses, pupils may be able to respond by means of a diagram, model, or drawing, by using gesture to indicate size, or by action such as mime, or by means of facial expressions. Where practicable, as in science or mathematics assessment tasks, they may be able to respond in mother tongue. This can be supportive if they have had the chance to use this during the relevant learning activities.

If bilingual support teaching can be provided, research has shown that many benefits accrue for the learners:

> In summary [these are] confident happy children; consciousness and pride in being bilingual; equal access to school concepts through two

languages; recognition of home culture; continuity between home and school; maintenance and extension of home language skills and development of a good command of English. (Jupp *et al*. 1988/9)

The additional benefit is, as the Schools Examination and Assessment Council (SEAC) Orders, 1990 make clear, that where this is available, there is no bar to using the Home language for explanations and assessment, except for assessing English (Assessment arrangement order 1990, KS1).

For the majority of bilingual pupils, however, their school acquisition of concepts and knowledge has to be through English, and so the language of assessment must be English. The SEAC Handbook of Guidance for SAT (Section Eleven) stresses the importance of children being made to understand, through every means at the teacher's disposal, what they are required to do. Teachers may find it useful to learn to ask 'Do you understand?' *in the child's mother tongue*. Other useful provisions may be:

- the provision of more visual support;
- longer time to carry out a task;
- using the language of instruction in the classroom well before the actual assessment;
- giving the child a chance to work on a one to one basis with the class teacher or language support teacher;
- provision of some culturally familiar materials for the assessment;
- setting the task in the context of the pupil's cultural and personal experience.

More specific supportive measures may be taken in relation to particular areas for assessment. For instance, it is permitted to use the recommended books for the assessment of Reading for shared reading beforehand. This is an opportunity to introduce some of the same stories in dual texts where available. Parents can play a part in translating some of the stories, and reading them to the children alongside the class teacher. A library of tape recorded stories in a range of languages can be built up as a school resource.

There is a danger that the focus on English, rather than Language, in the National Curriculum, may ignore broader language development in all its richness. However, references can be found which are supportive of a broader approach. For instance, in the programmes of study for Speaking and Listening, there are mentions of the use of stories, rhymes, poems and songs from different cultures. Reading attainment target Level 1(a) is 'recognise that print is used to carry meaning'. This gives an opportunity to arrange for children to hear stories being read from other scripts, so that they can be aware that a range of different symbols have equivalent value. Use of books from a range of cultures, such as the Chinese story *Chen Ping* and stories from the Asian culture such as *The Runaway Chapatti* and *The Old Woman and the Rice Thief* can successfully supplement the familiar English stories.

By means of simple measures like these, teachers can provide an instant link between home and school for young learners, and assist the process of giving them access to the sometimes culturally unfamiliar world of school.

In fact, the most valuable factor is every teacher's growing awareness of the particular learning needs and specific strengths of young bilingual pupils. Teachers with this awareness who devise ways to engage these bilingual pupils in the classroom learning opportunities and assessments are helping to make fuller curriculum access and fairer curriculum assessment achievable goals.

PART TWO:

Stories and Books

CHAPTER 7

Retelling Stories in School

Tony Aylwin

What's in a story?

There was once a woman who had four daughters, Lily, Filambo, Filanbetan and the youngest, Cacarat. Now she was kind to the three eldest girls, but Cacarat was scolded and given all the dirty jobs in the house to do.

Each morning their mother would go to market telling her daughters to lock themselves in the house and not to come out until she returned. When she did come back with food from the market, she sang:

> Lily, Lily, come here,
> Filambo, come here,
> Filanbetan, come here,
> But Cacarat, stay there.

And the three eldest daughters would run out of the house and eat up the food, so that Cacarat was given only the left-overs.

One day a giant was hiding near the house and overheard the mother's song. Next morning when she was at the market, the giant came to the house and sang in a high-pitched voice:

> Lily, Lily, etc.

The three eldest daughters ran outside thinking their mother was there with the food, but the giant snatched them up and put them in his sack. Then he went away.

When their mother returned from market, she sang the song as usual:

> Lily, Lily, etc.

But no-one came running out.

When she went inside to see what was the matter, Cacarat told her what had happened. Her mother was angry and tried to blame Cacarat at first. But when she realised that the others would not come back, she began to be kinder to Cacarat, and so they were able to live happily together.

Pamela Phillips, a First Year B.Ed student at Thames Polytechnic in Autumn 1990, shared this story with her group. Like her fellow students, she had been given the task of finding a traditional story to learn and tell in school. Having read through several collections of folk tales, she suddenly recalled the giant story from her childhood days in Dominica.

Although my written version does not do justice to her oral telling, several features should be clear. The story has a humble central character who, Cinderella-like, does the dirty work and gets no thanks for doing it. The favoured daughters suffer for their greed when, like the kids in Grimms' 'The Wolf and the Seven Little Kids', they are deceived by the giant. The giant, like many other monster figures, puts his victims into a sack. Like the sisters in Grimms' 'Ashputtel', they have no happy ending. This gruesome feature alarmed several of the group who expressed doubts as to whether Pamela should tell the story to the group of reception infants she was to work with the following week. Nevertheless, she went ahead and told the children the story as she had remembered it. The children received it well, but afterwards, when she had encouraged them to draw a scene from the story, she noticed that one boy had drawn the giant's sack with a hole in it, and four children were shown running away. He explained to Pamela that the three eldest daughters were escaping back home. The fourth escaping figure, he said, was a little boy who had been captured by the giant earlier at another house.

So the five-year-old boy solved the problem of the gruesome ending in his own way. I have since, with Pamela's permission, told the version with the boy's ending to a class of reception infants in another school, so the creole language story from Dominica is travelling on as all good stories should.

The choice of this story is also relevant to this chapter in other ways. Pamela, a mature student with children of her own, is an example of those parents who are resources when we are looking for stories that come from ethnic groups which are contributing to the make-up and development of contemporary British culture. Such stories have an added importance for children when they realise that their cultures are recognised and valued in school. Their eyes light up when they hear a story that they already know from home. Experiencing a wide variety of traditional stories will demonstrate the rich diversity of humanity in the world. At the same time, a growing familiarity with such stories from around the world will reinforce our sense of the common ground that is shared by all peoples.

Pamela's story also actively involves the children in the telling, particularly in the refrain. With younger children such features are very popular, both in stories from the European tradition (e.g. 'I'll huff and I'll puff and I'll blow your house down!') and from other cultures (e.g. 'I am the long one. I eat trees and trample on elephants. Go away, or I will trample on you!' from Verna Aardeema's East African story *Who's in Rabbit's House*?).

This sort of participation is very helpful when it comes to retelling by the children, and the chanted repetitions will be heard in their play. How to influence their own storytelling will be discussed as we proceed, but some observations about pre-school children and reception infants are needed first.

Storytelling in children's play

In her most recent book, Vivian Paley (1990) describes her work with very young children as they act out in their play the stories they tell.

> It is play, of course, but it is also story in action, just as storytelling is play put into narrative form.

She finds that children have a natural sense of putting thought and feeling into story form, and sees the giving of considerable time for play as vital if children are to develop in their learning.

> Any approach to language and thought that eliminates dramatic play, and its underlying themes of friendship and safety lost and found, ignores the greatest incentive to the creative process.

Such warnings may help us to be bold in encouraging explorations through play of stories like the Dominican giant story.

Another important formative feature develops when children play together. Paley says:

> The moment several children combine their imaginings, however, group instinct mandates a more conscious organization. Now the children insist upon rules, demanding of one another intense concentration, contemplation, comparison, interpretations, and self-evaluation. Characterizations must ring true, and scenes are required to look and sound authentic.

In such collaborative play, some children come with more experience of how to structure a story. What the children learn from each other, therefore, relates also to what each brings from home.

The influence of the home

Martin Hughes (1990) gives an account of a remarkable five-year-old Travellers' child, Sonnyboy, who demonstrates a mastery of the art of storytelling. His version of 'The Enormous Pumpkin' includes references to dogs and horses which feature importantly in his home culture, a point which probably will not surprise those with Traveller children in their classes.

> A long, long time ago there was this old man and he grew a pumpkin. And it was a very magic sort of pumpkin, cos when he went to get it up it was very, very big and enormous lookin'. He called for his man to give him a hand at pullin' it, but that was no use. So then he called for his boy and the biggest one o' his girls, and he said to them, PULL, PULL – it was no use again. So after a bit he thought and he thought and he thought about what he can do. Then he thought about his dogs and they had sharp teeth and they could hold on tight and PULL, PULL, dogs – but the dogs started fightin' and they all let go their tails and was bitin'. The man went mad at them then and got his fine horses and they was stronger 'an anyone in the world. They can pull a big wagon – PULL, PULL – horses can pull, and they did . . . and the old man had his pumpkin for supper and so did his man and all the children.

Martin Hughes assures us of the high quality of Sonnyboy's command of his audience through his use of voice, gestures, pauses and intonation. What is evident from the written transcript is his confident structuring of the story. Here is a child who is already experienced in hearing and retelling stories at home.

The Traveller community is strong in its storytelling tradition. So too are most of the cultural groups whose members have moved to Britain in recent years. Children whose families originate in Bangladesh, Nigeria and the Caribbean would be typical of such groups. Teachers, then, should seek ways of discovering and using the stories already known by the families whose children attend their schools. In some parts of the country parental involvement in story-telling has been achieved where LEAs have supported special projects, such as those in Tower Hamlets and Redbridge where the professional storyteller Mary Medlicott has run workshops to develop skills and confidence in parents who go on to tell stories in their children's schools.

The stories brought from home may include personal family ones, and there is clearly a case for encouraging these. Nevertheless, the traditional folktale has characteristics which give it special value. As Sonnyboy's retelling shows, the folktale is notable for its strong structure. This is a cross-cultural feature, and it is through their grasp of structure that we can help children develop a more profound appreciation of folktales. From using stories familiar to the children, teachers can go on to build a repertoire of multicultural stories.

The influence of the teacher

Young children's experience and understanding of story even before they have begun school has been found by research to be the most significant predictor of later educational achievement (Wells 1986). Such findings may make teachers feel somewhat helpless. With that thought in mind, Moyra Pickering (1989) set out to see if telling traditional folktales to five-year-old infants would improve their understanding of story.

At first Moyra asked the children individually, either on their own or with a friend, to tell her a story. Two examples of children clearly different in literacy development will illustrate the dramatic effect of her storytelling. Craig was a rather quiet boy with some problems in social interaction, whereas Rebecca had already made good progress in reading and writing.

Craig's first 'story':

> I was on my own and I saw little . . . (pause) . . . I saw bits and pieces and I saw . . . then I made a robot and I don't know what to make the eyes out of. Then . . . I saw everything and then I saw apples. Then I ate an apple . . . Then I saw a duck . . . Then I saw little wavy lines like, see those little wavy lines (points to Moyra's jumper) . . . Then I saw a pig in some mud and it squirted some water and it was splashing in some mud. Then I saw a little bit of my robot and I saw a little bit of glass, a bit of round glass, two bits of round glass and I needed them for my robot. And I cut . . . That's the end of the story.

Rebecca's first 'story':

> A puppy wanted a friend and had some dinner and after that she sat on a chair watching telly and after that she listened to the children's radio and sat on the settee to play games on the settee with her friend. That's the end.

Neither child responds with a story. Craig's reply seems to be about how to make a robot. In wondering what to make the eyes from he names a succession of objects that he can see in the classroom. Rebecca, after a more promising start about a lonely puppy, simply gives an account of how she spends an afternoon at home.

For the following five weeks the children had a regular input of stories told (not read) to them. After that they were asked to tell another story to Moyra. This time all the children told stories that were clearly structured and recognisably influenced by traditional stories. Craig tells, this time without hesitation, a story in which the villain is defeated by the combined efforts of the good characters. Rebecca devises a story in which characters interact, trickery is incorporated with wit and the whole has a satisfying framework. Craig's second story:

> Once upon a time there lived a mole in a hole. And a witch came along and threw a slimy cake at the mole's hole. And an elephant came along and the elephant sucked the slimy cake up from the hole and the elephant spat the slimy cake at the witch. And they ran and the monkey came and whacked it in the witch's face. And they all lived happily ever after.

Rebecca's second story:

> Once upon a time there was a fairy. She was a very nice fairy. She went over to the cupboard and she had to get her wand and that's why she had to go over to the cupboard. And she opened the door and she got her wand. She went over to the box. She opened the lid and she said, 'Abracadabra splosh!' And then all the toys turned into animals and then she said, 'Go over to that cupboard . . . you see that wand?' They went over to that cupboard (she hid it behind her back) and she ranned away as fast as she can. And then the animals rounded at her and then she flew off out of the sky to fly and then the animals ran down the path quickly as they can. One of them was a dragon, a big dragon. He blew his breath fire at her dress, and the fairy flied very fast and she turned round at the animals. She said, 'Abracadabra splosh!' and all the animals turned into toys again.

It is clear from this research that the stories that children hear at school also influence their own general understanding of story. Which stories carry most influence also needs to be considered. Like Pamela Phillip's Dominican story, Moyra's choice of stories, which included 'Tam Lin' and 'The Tinder Box', may not be everybody's idea of what is appropriate for five year olds to hear. Such stories remind us that memorable stories deal with powerful emotions, indeed are about emotions. When Fair Janet enters the forbidden forest of Carterhaugh to meet Tam Lin, she is both journeying into the depths of herself and towards the unknown world outside. The storyteller who understands this will convey its importance in the telling. The child who has heard enough stories will feel the significance of Janet's action, for it relates to Goldilocks and other folktale figures who decide to risk venturing beyond the safe world of their home surroundings.

Bettelheim (1976) sees such stories as a preparation for later life. Their importance to the individual is made clear in the work of Alida Gersie (1990, 1991) with emotionally disturbed adults. By using traditional folktales in her 'storymaking' approach to therapy, Gersie provides a framework in which life's problems are resolved, something which is not happening in life itself for these people. Sharing folktales with young children, then, seems likely to have long-lasting psychological benefits, but if a story is to make its effect on the children's understanding of life, it needs to be revisited many times.

Staying with the story

In a study based in a London Nursery School, Rosa Garrett (1991) closely observed the effect on children's language of staying with a story for a long time. She would tell a story herself many times, and provided books, jigsaws, pictures, puppets, clothing and objects for the play corner. Then she noted what happened. When she worked 'The Three Bears' in this way, Peter (4 years 8 months), who had been put on the 'at risk' register in the school, was transformed by the storytelling from a hesitant mumbler into someone who asked to be Daddy Bear in Rosa's Three Bears play for their parents in which he spoke clearly and confidently. Normally he asks questions like this:

Peter: Meat, more meat.
Staff member: More meat?
Peter: More meat, please.

Later, in a story (this time it is 'The Three Little Pigs'), he says: 'The little pig said, "Can I have some sticks, please?" ' The effect of the language of story on a child's linguistic ability is powerfully illustrated in Edie Garvey's book *Story as Vehicle* (1990). Although her book is largely about older children using English as a Second

Language, there is common ground with Garrett's study in her work with inexperienced users of the English language.

Jessica, a more able child than Peter, was recorded on three different occasions at monthly intervals retelling 'The Three Bears'. At 4 years 3 months she spoke very quietly and without expression:

> And Daddy Bear said, 'Who's been sleeping in my bed in my bed?'
> And Baby Bear said, 'Who's been sleeping in my bed?' And there she is.

In her second version, with Rosa as audience, she is more assured and clear about the story's structure as she 'reads' her own 'written' version. The third recording of Jessica, at 4 years 5 months, was made while she was engrossed in her own play. It has become a more elaborate telling:

> She went inside. First she tried Daddy Bear's porridge. Ugh! Too hot! Taste Mummy Bear's porridge. Too gooey! Tried Baby Bear's porridge. This was just right.

Because this story is so well known, it is likely that many of these children will have heard a version told at home, perhaps several times. What happens with equally powerful stories from other cultures, I suggest, is that there is not enough reinforcing or space made for revisiting the stories in play. Part of the problem seems to lie in the teacher's lack of familiarity with stories from other cultures, as well as feeling some reluctance to spend so much time learning new stories for telling rather than reading. Revisiting a story in the ways suggested above should reduce the number of stories used, but there is no doubt that some determined research is needed by the teacher if she is to discover the stories that mean most to her.

Finding good stories to tell

There is, of course, no shortage of good traditional stories in print and in out-of-print collections in libraries, and maybe the most satisfying results are had by those who are prepared to spend a lot of time trying to find stories that appeal to their particular tastes. Oxford University Press, The Penguin Folktale Library and Random House's Pantheon Folktale Library are just three examples of publishers who have wide-ranging lists of folktales.

However, to shorten the search, it may be advisable to start by consulting a guidelist, such as *The Books for Keeps Guide to*

Children's Books for a Multi-Cultural Society 0–7. Some 40 titles are commented upon in their section on Myths, Legends and Folktales, including picture books and collections of stories.

Two recent publications are of particular interest. Helen East's *The Singing Sack* (A. & C. Black, 1989) is a collection of stories from around the world, each of them containing a song. The accompanying audio-cassette includes the songs in their original languages. Rosalind Kerven's *Earth Magic, Sky Magic* (Cambridge University Press, 1991) is a collection of folktales from twelve different North American Indian peoples grouped around recurrent themes. Neither of these collections uses illustrations in the way that spoils so many collections of folktales. The best pictures are still those produced by the teller and the listener.

Despite the last comment, it is worth looking through children's picture books which are about single folktales. Some writers can be relied upon for good stories and memorable language in the retelling. Verna Aardeema is such a one. Her *Bimwili and the Zimwi*, for example, another monster and sack story, has fine opportunities for dramatic play and singing, as has Pete Seeger's South African story *Abiyoyo*.

Finally, the inspirational effect of having professional storytellers visit a school can be followed up by teachers and children retelling what they have heard and read. Storytellers such as Beulah Candappa, Grace Hallworth and Helen East have all written folktale collections with an emphasis on stories from around the world.

Concluding thoughts

When young childlren are given the time to experience a wide range of traditional stories in school through storytelling and dramatic play, the social and psychological benefits ought to be great. Quite why knowledge about stories seems so influential on educational achievement is less clear, though there is no doubt that linguistic ability is improved by familiarity with stories. But surely it has to be more than this. I am grateful to Ken Johnson (1991) whose study has helped to shape the following thoughts about this problem.

Folktales with their non-naturalistic features may give more opportunity for using imagination than other forms of literature. Imagination itself is a problematic concept, especially where educational achievement is being measured. Ted Hughes (1976) says:

The word 'imagination' usually denotes not much more than the faculty of creating a picture of something in our heads and holding it there while we think about it.

And, as Frank Smith (1990) says, the story form enables us to 'hold' ideas and feelings:

> Our prevailing propensity to impose story pictures on all experiences, real or imagined, is the ultimate governor of the imagination, the regulator that keeps it flying out of control.

So the teacher of young children, by making them familiar with the story form in its strongest folktale structures, is giving them access to using imagination which as Bruner (1986) says, 'is the basis of all science, literature, and philosophy – and of everyday experience and the "self" as well.' Stories, then, may be claimed to be of vital importance to all forms of learning. As Margaret Meek (1991) says:

> From the stories we hear as children we inherit the ways in which we talk about how we feel, the values which we hold to be important, and what we regard as the truth. We discover in stories ways of saying and telling that let us know who we are . . . We not only thrive on stories; we also survive by telling and retelling them, as history, discovery and invention.

CHAPTER 8

Choice of Initial Reading Material

Maura Blackburn

The nature of the books provided in school to support children learning to read is currently at the centre of a much publicised debate, one that concerns mono and bi-lingual children alike. Although it has taken a long time for teachers to build up bi-lingual expertise, it needs saying from the outset that general reading theory is applicable equally to the bi-lingual child and to the mono-lingual. The fact is, however, that the nature of the reading materials used in schools depends not necessarily on well formulated and generally agreed linguistic policy with its basis in undisputed research findings but, often, is more likely to be the result of decisions taken by a head teacher in past years. These decisions were often based mainly on financial expediency, or well meaning attempts to bring the school up to date by introducing a new system. Over the last twenty years, however, a slow evolution has been occurring, evidenced by the variety of approaches that can now be experienced in different school establishments.

As a result, the books sent home by teachers could be somewhat out-dated readers, more recently published readers, a mixture of these plus some specifically chosen 'story books', or simply any story book generally available in the school. The children could be able to choose from a wide selection of reading material, from within a specific ability level (often colour coded), or may be expected to read from a scheme only in strict rotation, progressing from easier to harder as each book is considered completed by the teacher. This, in itself, could appear haphazard to an observer; and any teacher unaware of such complexities of available choice might well assume that the particular approach chosen by their school was correct and the best available for their pupils.

In respect of the bi-lingual pupil, a major step forward has been taken in that where selection criteria have been applied, these criteria are now seen to apply equally to mono-lingual and bi-lingual readers – a book that a mono-lingual child can enjoy and learn from will be equally acceptable to a bi-lingual, and vice-versa, if the criteria include multi-cultural considerations. This change has occurred on two fronts, one being a demystification of the needs of bi-lingual children that has grown simply from more experience of their needs, and the second from new understandings about the prime require-ments for all children to gain meaning from the books they are using.

However, what has been lacking in the debate is an over-view based on firm research findings, one that can put the current approaches in the U.K. in mainstream reading into context, and one that embraces the field of bi-lingualism. (The major problems in assessing the effects of the use of different reading methodologies are summarised by B. Stierer (*Language Matters*, 1990/91), but without mentioning the needs of the bi-lingual learner). So it is to be expected that teachers new to primary education may be feeling confused. A small survey of post graduate students that I have recently undertaken indicates that teacher training establishments themselves provide only 'a little' or no insight at all into the needs of the bi-lingual reader. Not surprisingly, even where providing such an insight is part of the training curriculum, once in school the students have noted major contradictions between it and school practice. Whether from their own observations or from mainstream reading theory they are clear, however, that they prefer a choice of approach and materials to suit the individual needs of the children and that both reading scheme materials and story books are appropriate to the bi-lingual child. But it is the questions raised by these competing notions of literacy, as noted by Stierer, that still need to be resolved and it is unfortunate that much current debate has been polarised into story-books *v.* reading scheme factions.

It is worth quoting Margaret Meek, well known for her support of story book reading. At an in-school meeting convened in February 1990, she addressed teachers on the use of books in a primary school and cleared one misconception often attributed to her, that children can learn to read using *any* book. In fact, she stated that books need to be chosen with very clear criteria and if this is done, structure does not need to be imposed by the teacher, it comes from within the book itself. The criteria she chose to mention were that the print must make sense, it should be 'effortless' fun and worth sharing and retelling.

Betty Root (1987) highlighted another area of uncertainty when she claimed that it was irresponsible to denigrate teaching techniques that have been found to achieve required goals and that problems arose where teachers were not allowed to use methods that worked best for them. She is also a signatory to the 'Balance' Manifesto (1990) that calls for a balance between different approaches.

With this kind of debate continuing, confusion is bound to affect both established and newly trained teachers. Well recognised is the kind of 'de-skilling' that can over-take teachers new to the primary field, when past experience is forgotten or dismissed within the new situation. Often inveterate readers themselves, once they enter the school environs and the accepted status quo, they can become detached from their own experience of reading, of what makes a good book and the knowledge that choice of such a book rests mainly on its content. In many schools it seems there is little opportunity, either, for children to develop this facility of choice, which they exercise freely but with no guidance outside the school.

The bi-lingual reader

Where does this place the bi-lingual pupil at the present time? As a starter, there is a clear rule-of-thumb – if a book or method is unsuitable for a mono-lingual child, then it will be even more unsuitable for a bi-lingual child. Any teacher gaining experience with such children in a multi-cultural classroom soon comes to view their developing bi-lingualism as a clear asset, for are they not simply children lucky enough to be developing their literacy in two languages? As our experience with bi-lingualism has increased, there is also a growing awareness of the presence of a two-way process. This is where teaching approaches that have, of necessity, had to develop to make the curriculum accessible to bi-lingual children, often prove of equal value to others. Central to this came the need to develop a clarity of presentation and teaching materials that are meaningful to the children. The evolution that has taken place (witness the choice of materials and approaches), is in no small part due to the growing number of bi-lingual learners that are present in our schools.

Schools have learnt, often the hard way, that any given group of children, mono-lingual or bi-lingual, is best helped with the realisation that they exist as individuals and, to this end, there is a need for differentiated teaching and learning strategies. In the field of reading, Pinsent (1988) notes a drawing together of various strands of research, (Bryant & Bradley, 1985; Clark, 1976; Goldstein, 1976; Ehri, 1979 and others). On the face of it, some of the research appeared to be showing contradictory evidence. However, Pinsent has shown that the variety within the findings could reflect the variety of development to be found within children. Briefly, some children will have an early aptitude for reading for meaning and an aptitude for rhyme and associated interest in sounds; some children will have one but not the other; and some children will need help to develop both aptitudes. Such variety is normal within any group of children and will, of course, apply equally to bi-lingual children.

The problem of inappropriate reading materials has also often been addressed. Over the last twenty years books in school have been correctly accused of racial bias either by omission or commission. Not only were non-white children and their families not represented, but stereotyping of male and female roles was evident. A quick look now at one of the newer reading schemes e.g. *Connections* or *Sunshine* and others, indicates that this lesson has been taken to heart and now more general concerns regarding the nature of reading schemes in general are being addressed.

Briefly, the central aim of many reading schemes is to provide and build up a core of words that children can recognise in their readers and eventually in isolation, mainly by repetition of use, but gradually increasing in number and variety. Even in recent years, there would have been little opportunity for teachers to deviate from a chosen school system, although teachers became aware of an artificiality and limitation within the published texts, particularly within the beginning reader levels. Alongside this, certain patterns of reading development have been noted. Children, in general, will look for clues to help them with unknown words and seem to have expectations that the print will approximate to natural, everyday speech. Commonsense seems to dictate that any books aimed at helping children learn to read should not pose any more difficulties than necessary – in effect there should be good links between picture and print; the books should contain the type of everyday language children are used to and, in particular, they should be meaningful to the child. The work of Smith (1978) and Goodman (1972), confirmed that gaining meaning held primacy over other considerations, and this understanding is now linked closely to other more generalised learning theory, that known as 'meta-cognition', wherein there is recognition that humans in general strive to make sense of new learning by calling on prior knowledge and experience (Olsen, 1984).

Bi-lingual research

The past tradition of teaching English as a foreign language was based on the use of graded materials, often in withdrawal groups, using rote learning. However, experience began to indicate that children learn not in simple linear progression but by weaving together and learning to use the language they have around them. Inputs come from many sources, radio, television, teachers and other adults and this diversity imparts important advantages (Hester, 1984).

These understandings pointed to the need for teaching approaches that meshed with the language children are developing for themselves. The work of Barnes (1976), and Labov (1977) and others, made us much more aware of the value of the social context in which children learn. The way in which new languages are acquired has recent research attached to it. Gumperz (1982) notes that simultaneous acquisition of both the first and second language is more familiar, but consecutive acquisition can occur. Here one language is established to a greater or lesser degree before a second is acquired. Teachers working within a multi-cultural environment will encounter a variety of second language backgrounds. Some children will speak no English at home; others will have parents who have good English but use their first language in the social context of their homes and friends whereas they use English in their external environment. Some children will have opportunity to develop their first language via Saturday school or schools attached to religious establishments. Children who are most likely to have limited experience of spoken English are children coming from homes where no English is used, and of course, very young children.

For people working within the multi-cultural education field the expectations have been that, following the initial period of non-English speaking parents and children entering school with little or no English, second generation children would have more exposure to English before school entry. However, with continued immigration, particularly from the New Commonwealth, and the maintenance of mother tongue use within home and community, we have noted a continued flow of children entering reception and other years with little or no English. The situation is, in fact, becoming more complicated because of an exodus of refugees from Somalia and other countries, with many city schools now having the status of being named as International Schools because of the variety of cultures represented in their pupils.

With young children, the development of general concepts in their first language parallels what they are able to achieve in the language they are newly acquiring; and, of course, a mismatch will occur if the learning required in school is not meaningful. Poor mother tongue development will, in fact, slow down second language acquisition. Mayor (1988) has noted that irrespective of linguistic background, children apply similar strategies to reading tasks – once children have developed concepts within their first language, this will aid development of their second language. Cummins and Swain (1986) note research showing that bi-linguals develop more analytic strategies and sensitivity to cues as a means of overcoming inter-lingual interference (Ben-Zeev, 1977, writing on Hebrew/English and Spanish/English bi-lingual acquisition). However, in the early stages they will be disadvantaged in the sense that they do not have access to the same cueing systems as the native speakers whose spoken language is closest to that of the written language.

A study by Goodman, Goodman and Flores (1979) has produced a profile of second language learners and the type of problems they experience. Central to this, and the aspect they believe teachers should have most concern for, is disruption to comprehension. Swain (1977) notes that findings over the last decade show that a second language is acquired, to a large extent, through the 'creative construction' of the new language by the learner – that is through the learner's systematic and gradual reconstruction of the rules of the language, where the focus of the speaker and listener is on the *message* being conveyed, not on the form of that message. Goodman and Smith both look to the construction of meaning and the use of syntactic knowledge as the principal components in reading, right from the start.

Observers of the debate concerning bi-lingual learning will be aware of the queries concerning first language instruction in school and the obvious advantages of teachers who are bi-lingual themselves. However, such debate, although important, can cloud the general issue of fast and efficient acquisition of a second language. For example Cummins and Swain (1986) note studies in French-speaking Canada and state that every study that has compared early total immersion in the second language, against core programmes (say 20/40 minutes daily concentrating on vocabulary and grammar), reveals significant differences in favour of immersion. Emerging from these studies is support for the hypothesis that context-embedded second language skills develop primarily as a function of exposure to the use of that language in the environment.

Teacher as a researcher

It is Monday morning. The children from a class of 6-7 year olds are rushing noisily in at the start of another busy school week. Most of them are clutching their reading books, happy in the knowledge that, with a little help from home, they have completed the reading task set by teacher on the previous Friday. What distinguishes this class from many others is that 99% of the children are from Asian families and there is a babble of communication occurring both in English and in Panjabi as the children chat to each other about their week-end experiences, act as interpreters for parents and grandparents, and generally show themselves to be established bi-lingual communicators.

Such a situation will, of course, be strange to many teachers in the U.K. Some newly trained teachers or teachers without a special interest or expertise in language may feel threatened by the unknown. Many people, both parents and teachers, probably view the reading book the child is returning as merely something to support the teacher in her linguistic approaches; a reading book is after all a fairly innocuous item, isn't it? The fact that the children are taking books home at all must surely indicate the priority given to reading within the school, not something to cause undue worry. Within an environment of so many intangibles and many unanswered questions, at least the reading is sorted out! But is this really so?

From all that has been written and said, there must be the clear message that in education the field of knowledge is never static, it is there to be explored, with opportunites for every teacher, experienced and inexperienced. In a small research project (Blackburn, 1990), I investigated what was happening to reading approaches for second language learners, and in particular attempted to find whether it was possible to quantify different outcomes to the use of a reading scheme or story books as teaching media.

A preliminary visit to a Junior school in the London Borough of Brent with four years experience of the story book approach, catering for a wide ethnic mix of children, indicated that they had developed explicit criteria for choice of materials. These were:

- Single line text
- Picture only (i.e. books of good illustrative quality that provide opportunity for discussion)
- Picture plus text (i.e. good links between the picture and the text)
- Accumulative text (e.g. 'I went shopping and I bought')

- Rhythm and poetry
- Different styles of print/book (to prevent stereotyping 'acceptable' book formats)
- Multi ethnic images/anti stereotypes (e.g. gentle boys, dominant girls)
- Folk/fairy tales from around the world
- Dual text relevant to school mix
- Fiction and non fiction
- Story cassettes

Visiting a further six schools, teaching 4–7 year olds, all with bilingual intake, I found a clear consensus that approaches should not be written in tablets of stone. In fact, teachers were experimenting with new approaches and their choice of reading materials had been affected by awareness of the shortcomings of reading scheme material and the positive promotion of the story-book approach. They were being more selective about the reading materials they were using. However, where methods were tried and tested and found to be successful, there was a marrying together of the old and the new, including phonic knowledge. So for example in schools still operating reading schemes, young emerging readers were given support by direction through early readers but were encouraged to expand out into wider selection once they achieved given proficiency. The schools taking on a story book approach were quick to recognize potential problems and were able to call on support staff to advise them. For example, parental involvement was seen as crucial and where parents expressed doubts, the schools undertook special sessions to put the parents in the picture. Where children were not picking up a core vocabulary from the story books used, specific emphasis was given to this in the writing the children were doing.

The main body of the research involved observing the reading process at work with two groups of bi-lingual learners, over a two year period. At commencement of the study the children, from two separate schools, were in reception classes, aged 4 + . They consisted of Panjabi speaking children, plus two boys from a Cantonese background. In one school the children were learning to read via the *Ginn 360* scheme, backed up by phonic teaching. In the other school, the children were given free choice, mainly from *Story Chest* books (a published scheme but with a wide vocabulary and emphasis on meaning), with more books to choose from as the school gradually acquired new resources. During the two year period the children were monitored for reading development. The non-standardised assessments used were running records of reading over three levels of difficulty, *Concepts about Print*, both adapted from Marie Clay (1972), her check on alphabetic awareness, analysis of reading error via the Goodman and Burke (1972) miscue procedure, and attitudinal assessment.

From the outset of the study it was clear that within both groups (as with any other children), each child was interacting with the reading process in his or her own personalised way. There were in both groups children who were naturally good readers, and children who were finding the process difficult. There were children who found it easy to use initial sounds to help them with an unknown word and those who found it difficult.

However, at the end of the two year study, analysis of reading errors over three levels of reading difficulty utilising the Goodman and Burke categories of reading error (miscue analysis), indicated a significant finding. On grapho-phonic miscue there was a difference between the two groups in favour of the reading scheme children. The Mann-Whitney method of statistical analysis indicated that this effect was very unlikely to occur by chance, (i.e. in only 5 cases out of 100 would results as extreme occur by random chance). This finding indicated that the reading scheme children looked more closely at the written words and had consolidated a core vocabulary. This compared with the story book children who at the end of the two years, as a group, were still mainly memorising the text. The story book group were better at supplying words correct for meaning when they tackled an unknown word but by not so large a margin.

At the end of the two years, the two groups were more or less on equal footing as regards their *Concepts about Print*, and their alphabetic awareness appeared linked to their individual reading development, that is, the more experienced the reader, the higher the score. Attitudinal responses showed that the reading scheme children's awareness of books was specifically linked to the books they took home as readers, although other books were available to them in school. The story book children as a group had a better awareness of the wider applications of reading and were clearer on the books they liked.

Implications from this study

Results from this study have clear implications for classroom pedagogy, and not only for bi-lingual learners. These concern the teaching of strategies to support children and those that involve the types of reading material offered. Within both groups, there were children in difficulty with the early stages of reading and it was clear there were other factors involved apart from reading material and classroom practice. For the individual teacher there is a crucial message – that *becoming your own classroom researcher is infinitely preferable to accepting theory and methodologies developed at another time and in another place.* Linked closely to this comes an awareness that time spent in looking more closely at children having specific problems will not only help the child but will upgrade your own working practice. Whatever procedures you investigate, they can be adapted to make them more practical in a busy classroom situation. (Note C. Moon's update on *miscue analysis*, 1991, which simplifies the procedure to analysis of substitution words only, these being considered the most informative).

The running record and miscue procedure provided insight not only into individual children as readers but also into the materials and teaching approaches used in the two study schools, over and above teacher anecdote. From their use it became clear that children do not exist in isolation as readers but the manner in which they inter-act with the print, the type of reading error made, really does provide 'windows' into the reading process but also into the child as a person. For example, you may find a child produces a scattered collection of reading miscues, covering all three categories, the semantic, the syntactic and the grapho-phonic thus confirming your classroom observations of limited concentration and a type of 'grass-hopper' learning, rushing from one task to another without consolidation.

For the bi-lingual child still developing spoken language, miscues will tend to be grouped under the syntactic heading if they have not fully developed their day to day use of spoken English or expectations of what the print might say. Here it is evident that if the material being read does not contain the type of natural language the children are used to hearing and using, extra difficulties will be put in their path and, of course, a strong programme for developing oracy is needed. Books with accumulative and repeating text are helpful in this case.

Obviously, again, where miscues are occurring under the semantic category (meaning), the reading materials need a critical look to see if they are actually conveying their message clearly. Any book that does not do this should be avoided. Clearly, if they provide clear meaning, if they are appropriate to the stage of reading development of the child but the child is experiencing reading difficulty, there may be problems with comprehension across the board. This is particularly crucial for bi-linguals. Usually, time and exposure to story-telling and reading, lots of discussion, particularly one-to-one, rhymes, songs, etc. will bring children forward with positive effects on their own reading.

Grapho-phonic miscue is an area that teachers observe as occurring frequently with both mono and bi-lingual children. At seven years of age, there will still be children in mainstream classes who are unable to recognise sounds consistently. These will include second language learners who are also having to cope with the rhythm and intonations of a new language and some may always retain those of their mother language when speaking English. The value or otherwise of a phonic programme has been the basis for debate and argument and schools have witnessed a decline in its practice. Those teachers who have maintained that it does have a part to play in reading development have, in general, adapted their approaches. Phonic drills and rote practice are now more likely to be replaced with one-to-one conferencing with the inexperienced reader as how best to tackle an unknown word. Whole class practice is most likely to be centred on word games and rhymes, poems and songs. What is clear is that in order to become fluent readers, children need the ability to recognise words they know but have yet to experience in print. It is at this stage they need to use their developing knowledge of the relationships between letters and sounds in words. My study seems to indicate that children being shown such relationships within the context of their reading, make fewer grapho-phonic errors. Some children seem to have this 'phonemic awareness' naturally; others will benefit from explicit instruction in letter-sound relationships.

The study did indicate some clear findings in favour of story books. The use of story books seemed to convey a particular advantage in that the children using them were being exposed to a variety of book formats, and this provided them with a wider base to their literacy – their meta-cognition was more developed. Additionally, the story-book children were at a slight advantage in providing alternative words that were correct for meaning, when they were unable to read the text. Presumably, this was facilitated by their exposure to a wider vocabulary, not necessarily words they could read at this stage. However, the expectations and knowledge of the reading scheme children were tied into their readers, these being the books they took home.

The perceived advantages of 'story' material allowing children to experience exciting vocabulary, clarity of meaning and also a structure from 'within' need not be seen as exclusive to 'stories'. Scheme material, if chosen with care, can combine these criteria in a way that many emerging readers will benefit from and clearly children in the study had consolidated an initial reading vocabulary. Crucial, however, is the manner in which the teacher chooses to use the books available to her. Change can be introduced overnight but *monitored* change, that is to everyone's benefit, needs to be class based and carefully executed.

Drawing together research findings and observed teacher practice indicates that versatility and diversity can enter any teacher's repertoire, whatever the reading materials available. Scheme material and story books have their own particular strengths that, with careful management and a clear philosophy of reading, can be passed to the young readers in our care.

CHAPTER 9

Selecting Literature for Young Children

Pat Pinsent

It is a common sensation, on completing a thesis or even an essay, to feel, 'That ties it up. I've looked at all the relevant literature on (for instance) children's cognitive development.' And then, six months later, out comes a revolutionary new book on the subject, and then a reply to that and a host of new articles in journals. Time is short, the effort to read all this new material and to keep up-to-date is hard to justify amid the demands of day to day teaching, and feelings are divided between joy that the subject remains in the public eye, and a tinge of resentment, 'Why do they have to keep on writing books?'

Nowhere is this truer than in the field of children's literature. Even reading reviews of the hundreds of books that are published each year is scarcely possible. Although later in this book we do provide a list of some books suitable for a multi-ethnic group of young children, my intention here is rather to help the teacher to be aware of factors which need to be borne in mind in selecting such books.

It is probably only since about 1960 that it has been true to claim that Britain is a multi-racial society. While for centuries there have been some black people in this country, it would be unrealistic to expect writers to have automatically depicted black characters in books set in Britain. In the last thirty years, however, the situation has totally changed, so that different standards need to be applied according to whether a book has been published recently or not.

The same care has of course to be exercised in using books published before this time, but their portrayal, or non-portrayal, of ethnic minority characters needs to be firmly set in period – a process which may be difficult or even impossible if they are read to or by children of the age-group with which we are concerned here. The immediate consequence of this is that some books may no longer be suitable for children of the age for which they were originally intended. Examining allegations of racism in Blyton's *Noddy* books, for instance, may be a very suitable activity for secondary school pupils but I would be sorry to see the books, at least in the old editions, used with the pre-school children who were their original audience.

Books published in this country today must address the fact that our society is no longer mono-lingual or mono-cultural. This does not mean that all books have to have token black or Asian characters, but rather that there should be no distortion of the make-up of the population, particularly of inner-city areas. Books which in their illustrations or their choice of names of characters provide an all white mono-culture should be regarded with suspicion – especially concerning their use in schools which do have an all white intake. It is my contention that schools which lack members of ethnic minorities have a responsibility to prepare their pupils for the real world of racial mix. Those who say, 'Racism is not our problem because all our pupils are white' have the biggest problem of all!

There are many books today which in a very casual way, through illustrations or the use of non-English names, succeed in incorporating children from different ethnic backgrounds. It is difficult to draw the line between tokenism and fidelity to a multi-racial mix, especially in books written about schools or set in urban localities. From the Ahlbergs' *Starting School* (1988), through the range of characters encountered in Shirley Hughes' Alfie and Annie Rose books (1988 etc.), Geraldine Kaye's *Small Street* series (1989/90), Margaret Joy's *Allotment Lane School* (1985), and Fay Sampson's *Chris and the Dragon* (1985), many recent books for young children make their settings a microcosm of today's society. The effect is to normalise the position of children from a minority group – they don't have automatically to identify with the child(ren) in the book who are of the same racial origin, but they are *there*.

Much recent research has emphasised the value of story. Harold Rosen (1988) in a postscript to Betty Rosen's book on story telling (largely in the secondary school) talks of how narrative is:

> a supreme means of rendering otherwise chaotic, shapeless events into a coherent whole, saturated with meaning. (p. 164)

He quotes Bruner (1986), who claims:

> There are two modes of cognitive functioning, two modes of thought, each providing distinctive ways of ordering experience. The two (though complementary) are irreducible to one another. Efforts to

ignore one at the expense of the other inevitably fail to capture the rich diversity of human thought.

Rosen continues with showing how the 'paradigmatic', or 'logico-scientific' mode of thought, which tends to predominate in school, at least with older children, needs to be supplemented by the 'narrative' mode. In narrative, two landscapes are constructed simultaneously, 'the landscape of action' and the 'landscape of consciousness', where we encounter the feelings of those involved in the action.

Fiction, through the centrality it gives to plot and character, provides something which the child cannot derive from factual writing alone. It is not enough, therefore, to provide books which present in a non-fiction framework the details of, for instance, Sikh or Muslim life in Britain. Such books, well intentioned as they no doubt are, will not help children to know from the inside what it is like to *be* a child with a different cultural background from their own. Narrative will be the best means of doing this.

It's worth reminding ourselves that children at school in this country come from a very wide range of racial, cultural and linguistic origins. It is too easy to use the word 'black' to mean any people whose ancestors were not European, and to forget that, for instance, children whose parents or grandparents are West Indian will often find Asian customs as difficult to understand as the indigenous children do.

Literature derives some of its most potent effects from allowing children to identify with those who have had different experiences, whether of events or of emotions. Extension of sympathies by putting the readers into the position of someone apparently unlike themselves who nevertheless seems to have so much in common with them can be one of the most powerful ways of countering prejudice. It is therefore particularly important that not too many of the ethnic minority characters in books for young children should be portrayed as under-privileged victims of society. It is better to generate in the indigenous children experiencing the story a feeling of empathy with black characters than to cause them to feel pity for them, an emotion not always compatible with respect. The effect on the self-image of the black child as a result of the experience of stories where black people are constantly seen as underprivileged also needs careful consideration. It is just as important to provide children with role-models of active and interesting black and Asian characters as it is to avoid stereotyping girls as passive. It is of course equally important that ethnic minority characters should not be unbelievably good!

It is debatable whether it is desirable to confront children below Junior school age with the literary experience of racism, even though many children may have already had to encounter it in real life. Material which shows children being racially abused can be double-edged – to young children it may appear to legitimate, by putting into writing, some of the racist terms they have heard but possibly not fully understood. If such books are read by young children, the situation may need careful handling by the teacher or parent. I think it's more immediately helpful at this stage to use stories which have as central characters children who are obviously of some minority group, such as Afro-Caribbean, Asian or Chinese, and show them going through the same kind of experiences as any other child. An interesting approach is that of Jamila Gavin, herself of mixed race, in *Kamla and Kate* (1983), where two girls, one Indian, one English, aged six, are neighbours. Through their naive remarks, differences in culture are explored. For instance, when each of them in turn goes to tea with the other, both complain that they don't like the food and land up eating chocolate biscuits instead.

A valuable perspective all too rare in books for children of any age is that of the multi-racial family. Tony Bradman and Eileen Browne, in *Wait and See* (1988), present Jo, the daughter of a white father and black mother. This is a book which incidentally also reverses gender stereotypes by showing the father in a caring role.

The books which I have mentioned so far are from the genre of realistic fiction rather than that of fantasy. In fact, there seems to be a tendency for books dealing with social matters, not surprisingly, to be in a realist mode, while fantasy tends to relate more obviously to psychological, philosophic and religious themes. Nevertheless, there can, I think, be a role for fantasy in the area of anti-racism, particularly in the hands of a teacher who is alert for opportunities. One of the most frequently used types of fantasy for this age range is the folk and fairytale; since these are available from so many different cultures, there are clear opportunities for displaying the variety of heritages available, and also the similarities between tales from different backgrounds. There is some danger however in too unmixed a diet of folktales as the main means of multi-cultural teaching. Some children may be bored by them, and what is potentially more serious, these stories inevitably locate children of particular racial backgrounds in foreign countries. The teacher's role is vital here, in showing the universality of the tales.

The other main variety of fantasy for young children is the animal story, generally of an anthropomorphic kind. Most of these are fairly neutral, and it is easy to see why writers unsure about the portrayal of ethnic identity may feel on safe ground with animals! Nevertheless, if the animals in the story are shown as too exclusively favouring their own species, or, indeed, if certain species (such as rats or spiders) are shown as stereotypically evil, a subliminal message of speciesism may come through, which at least is not doing the cause of anti-racism any good. Conversely, the many animal stories for young children which show inter-species toleration (such as John Burningham's *Mr Gumpy's Outing* (1970)) or emphasise respect for the individual (as in David McKee's *Elmer* (1989) where an elephant who is different because he is patchwork in colour is shown as highly popular) may be, with unobtrusive comment, a valuable means of leading children towards acceptance of those who are from different backgrounds.

Many sets of guidelines against racism have been issued, for instance Dixon (1977), Klein (1985), about how to judge the presentation of characters, language and themes in children's books. I am not convinced, however, that some of these writers place enough importance on the quality of the writing. It seems to me that poorly written books, however well intentioned, can easily do more harm than good. Books which are written solely to combat racism, by writers whose use of English is such that it would not be tolerated if they were writing on any other subject, may antagonise children, or, at the very least, may bore them. I would hope that books for young children, whatever their theme, would have some of the qualities advocated by writers such as Margaret Meek (1988). They should, for instance, work at two or more levels, so that there is a depth which children respond to even if they do not fully understand it. Picture books particularly need not 'talk down' to either the reader or the listener.

Paradoxically, I think there is also a need for anti-racism in books which are *not* quality fiction. As Dickinson (1970) points out, there is a need for 'rubbish' to form part of children's reading, and it is important that non-quality writing should not foster intolerance. Unfortunately, many of Blyton's books, for all ages, reveal outdated attitudes towards the outsider, and even Dahl's work has been open to censure. The world of comics too has not, I think, been given enough scrutiny for its racial attitudes though its sexism is already well known! Since this kind of material is less likely to be discussed in class than the kinds of books I have mentioned, it is an area which is more likely to pass with its attitudes uncorrected. I am certainly not advocating censorship here, but I think that schools should do as much as they can in the way of providing parents with information about books which are undemanding as well as those which are educational, and perhaps providing these too in school bookshops. Teachers might also try to be alert to the unrecognised messages conveyed by comics and similar material for young children.

A study of children's literature of the past reveals that it has always been didactic – the teaching aims have varied, and the explicitness of the teaching has generally diminished over the years, but it would be idle for most children's writers to claim that their intentions were solely to entertain children. The writer's values will come out, either explicitly or implicitly. The communication of these to children today is probably far more effective if the mode is implicit. All the more reason, then, for the literature provided by the school, whether as material read by the children or as stories read or told to them, to be very affirmative in its attitudes towards those of different cultural and ethnic groups.

There are then a number of strategies for teachers to employ in choosing literature to support an anti-racist school policy. Plenty of well written and illustrated books need to be provided, the choice perhaps helped by teachers or parents of different races if they are available for consultation. Books which because of changed attitudes in society demand too much putting into historical perspective can be avoided. Issues like these can be tactfully brought into the open where they are relevant but otherwise implicit. Parents can be supplied with lists of non-racist or anti-racist fiction, and, where possible, given the chance to buy it in the school. All these approaches I think are better than censorship. Children need to be able to grow up to make their own choices, which will ultimately mean that they need to be able to reject racist attitudes, whether they occur in books, comics, on television or in real life. The teacher, by choosing and using books, must be a facilitator of that process.

PART THREE:
Active Language Users

CHAPTER 10
Children's Developmental Writing

Peta Lloyd

Throughout England, especially in urban areas, children are entering schools with a first language other than English. Some of these children will use English as well as their first language within their home or community. Most will watch some English television and will have some implicit knowledge of print in the environment, which may be in more than one script. Some may have had experience of writing at home. However in many cases, especially in areas where there are large communities where a language other than English is used, children will come to school in the position of having to use the English language for communication for the first time. They will also be expected to develop reading and writing skills in an unfamiliar language. Their position in this respect will be different from their monolingual peers whose reading and writing development will be built upon an already well developed spoken repertoire of English.

In order to investigate children's early writing development, I worked with Chris Norris, a reception class teacher in Featherstone First School, Southall. All the children in her class, excepting one, were bilingual. Chris's approach is child centred. She tries to build on the children's early experience of print. She is well aware of the inter-relationship between the development of talk, reading and writing and knows a lot about writing development, which is important in order to be able to understand the process the children are going through. In the light of Chris's practice we looked at issues surrounding the development of writing and how best to facilitate writing with young bilingual children.

How can you help the children to feel at home?

It is important to develop the right classroom ethos to begin with.

Chris tries to make the classroom reflect the children's home backgrounds as much as possible. The class teacher may not be able to speak the children's home language but she can compensate a little for this by providing taped stories in home languages and dual text books or books in a range of languages. Signs and labels can be written in a range of scripts and teachers can collect book, pictures and artefacts reflecting children's cultures. Parents or other adults speaking children's first languages can also be invited into the class to work with groups of children.

What should the room look like in order to facilitate the writing process?

Chris's classroom is organised into different areas to facilitate an integrated day. The areas include those set aside for role play, art and craft, construction, maths and science, as well as the writing corner. Each area has resources available to aid independence in the learning process. The writing area is bright and light with a resource base full of pencils, crayons, felt tips, rulers, rubbers, different types and sizes of paper, some 'books' already stapled together, a stapler, paper clips, simple picture dictionaries, sellotape and anything else that can be used to stimulate the writing process, such as signs or wall charts. It is important that children have somewhere to display or put their work when it is finished. This might be a display board at their own level, or, if they don't want to display a piece of work, a box to put it in. Although this is the main writing area, writing is encouraged in all areas of the classroom, for example, if the role play area was a café then menus would be made and pads and pencils provided to take orders from the 'customers'.

Where do you start when the children arrive at school?

Many of the children arriving in Chris's class have had some nursery experience where they would have been used to operating in a predominantly English-speaking setting. However for a small minority of children school may be a new and daunting experience. Chris likes to ascertain from the beginning what the children know about writing and one way of doing this is by encouraging them to write and looking at what they produce, remembering a process model starts with the child. Children are encouraged to write in their first language as well as English if they wish. Doing this is particularly stimulated if they see other scripts around them, if these scripts are discussed, or if they see adults writing in other scripts. The early example of Harinder's writing in Panjabi shows that she is familiar with more than one script (Example 1). Her parents are keen for her to become literate in Panjabi as well as English and are encouraging her to recognise Panjabi letters.

Example 1.

I read with my sister a book.

Example 2.

'Giant walking'

Some children may have a wide experience of print in more than one language. They may also have a rapidly increasing knowledge of story and have already started to write, whereas others may have very little previous literacy experience. Manpreet's first piece of writing, produced at the beginning of October, was in response to a story about a giant (Example 2). Young bilingual children starting school may find it difficult to describe in English what they are drawing. Talking to children individually about their work is time consuming but very necessary. Manpreet told Chris she had drawn 'giant walking'. Further discussion will allow Manpreet to hear whole sentences describing the giant and to refer back to the story. Sometimes Chris will add a sentence under the child's work which will be read together initially and perhaps shared with the whole class. Manpreet is using some letters from her name, is writing from left to right across the page and is developing the concept of words as can be seen by the spaces in her writing.

Why is talk important in the writing process?

Chris says that from the beginning she bathes the children in English, both oral and written. Talk always precedes writing in the classroom and the talk is always supplemented with concrete objects, pictures or books in order for all the children to understand as much as possible of the discussion, if there is no bilingual support available. Every activity has a practical foundation. Children are encouraged to describe events, retell stories, explore problems, pose questions and find solutions. Discussion amongst the children may be in first languages. Chris encourages children to report back in larger groups and to the whole class in English. Any discussion feeds in new vocabulary and English structures which can then be used in writing.

How do you develop purposes and audiences for children's writing?

Written English is role modelled at every opportunity in order to illustrate the purpose of writing. For example, notes from other teachers are read together and answers are composed together. Chris's aim is to demonstrate the importance of writing, by using and discussing it with the children. Stories play an important part in this process and are read in the morning and afternoon. Children become authors from the beginning. Chris scribes and makes books with the children in groups. These books then become part of the book stock and can be read in the class and also taken home. Older children in the school often join the class for 'book time' after dinner and read to small groups and individuals.

In February, Sunil wrote his first book (Example 3). Sunil is a very interested and enthusiastic writer whose spoken English is developing rapidly. He loves stories and this is seen to be reflected in his story writing. He draws on ideas from stories he knows and uses his familiarity with the language of story in his own writing. Sunil wrote and drew the first five pages of his story and showed them to Chris. He read the story to her and they talked about the content and the ending that Sunil wanted to write. When he got to page 5, Sunil had difficulty in reading what he had written, because of his layout on the page. Chris showed him how to put dots down the left hand side of a page, as a reminder of where to start each line. Sunil used this idea, when he wrote the last page of the story. Chris and Sunil also

Example 3, page 1

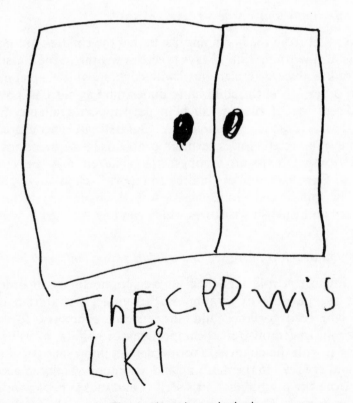

The cupboard was locked.

Example 3, page 2

The cupboard was locked but a little bit open.

Example 3, page 3

There was a teddy bear.

discussed the spelling of 'was', which he had written correctly on a previous occasion and he substituted an 'a' for the 'i' on page 5 and spelt the word correctly on page 5. Sunil was the first in the class to attempt to write a story in book form. Chris helped him to mount his work and make it into a hard-wearing book. She also supplied a printed 'interpretation' of the story, to enable others to read it. Sunil read his book to the class, took it home to show his parents and then it was put into the book corner, where it was read by other children both in school and at home. It prompted other children to begin making books by themselves.

Example 3, page 4

Example 3, page 5

Out of the window there was a white moon.

Other genres are not neglected. Children are encouraged to be aware of, and write in different styles from the beginning. Chris and the children produce a monthly newspaper that is much read. The role play area is used to demonstrate written genres such as list and letter writing. Kulwant wrote this letter in the 'post office' to Lee, a temporary nursery nurse who had been working with the class the previous week (Example 4). After writing the letter, she read it to Chris who then collected other letters the children had written and

HE SCRDaM

He SORDaM

ToCLi . mummy

ThE ar

. NThe ih YRi RoM
. waS a raLRCa
                 HRS
                   o
. DaBHe isfLa Na
. cindeRella pmy Dos

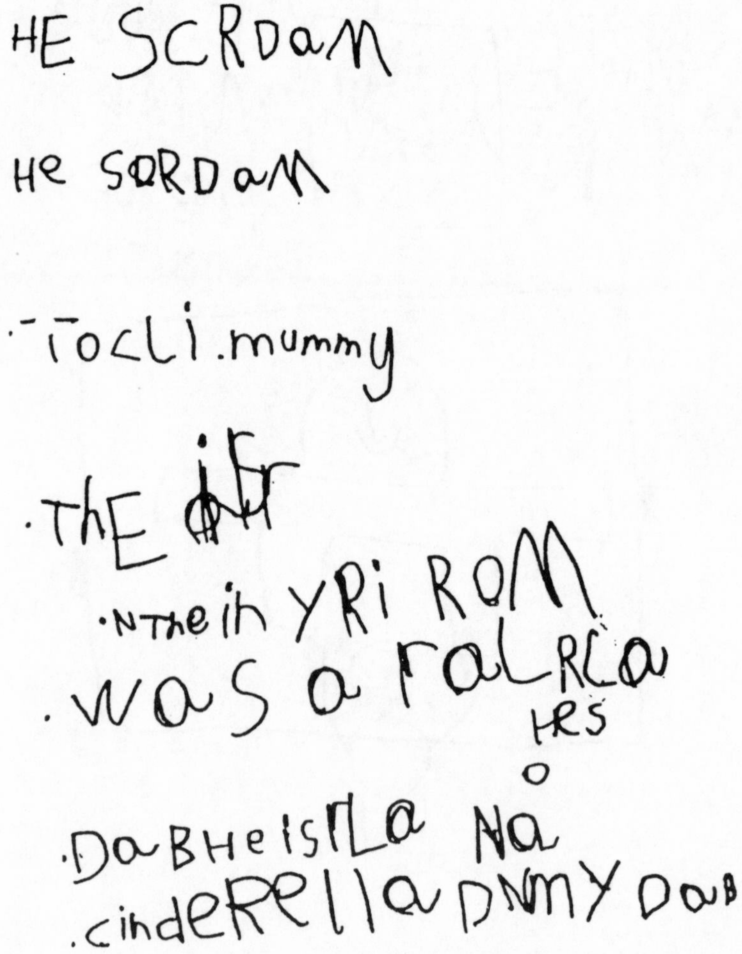

He screamed. He screamed to call mummy. There is nothing in your room. It
was a real teddy bear. Cinderella turned my teddy bear, now he's real.

posted them to Lee. Lee replied to the children individually and they
were extremely proud of the letters they had received, which they read
to each other. Mathematical and scientific observations are shared in
a whole class group and may be written up by Chris, helped by the
children, or later in the year by pairs or individual children. In June
Monica, a bilingual child, recorded her scientific observations about

Example 4.

Dear Lee,
I hope you have a nice time at home.
love from Kulwant.

Example 5.

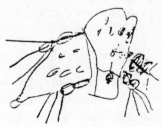

First we had some mum and dads. He had some baby eggs. The baby egg grows into frogs.

the tadpoles the class had collected and watched grow into frogs (Example 5). The class had regularly observed and talked about what was happening to the tadpoles. This discussion had provided Monica with the English necessary to do this piece of writing. She has used posters, books and labels around the room to help with spellings and has drawn lines to show where she is having difficulty with a word. In this way she can finish her piece of writing, concentrating on content, and then talk to Chris about what she has said and also the words that she is not yet able to spell. Enabling children to focus on the content of their writing is important for all children, but especially important for young bilingual children who may be working in a language that does not yet flow comfortably and where a lot of concentration is needed.

What about the secretarial aspects of writing?

Chris encourages children to look, from the beginning, at how words are spelt. This process starts with discussion about their names and includes naming and recognising the sounds of initial letters. When Chris scribes for individuals or groups of children, she encourages them to tell her how to spell words. Simple word games are used in odd five minutes to make spelling fun. Words related to work in progress are discussed, modelled and then usually found on the wall in a display or with work relevant to the topic. Later in the year, children are encouraged to use picture dictionaries or books from the book corner if they know these contain a word they want to use in their writing. Encouraging children to be confident in their attempts at spelling is important.

Talking about handwriting and the correct formation of letters takes place in a similar way. As writing is modelled so the formation of letters is discussed. Children practise handwriting regularly and are shown how to form letters correctly. This takes place in small groups with Chris nearby to make sure letters are being written correctly and children are not developing bad habits. Handwriting practice and 'real writing' are seen as two separate and different activities.

How do you assess children's progress in writing?

Chris monitors children's progress throughout the year by talking to the children about their work and collecting and analysing samples. In this way a picture can be built up of the children's progress.

Diagnosis can be made as to where the children may be having problems, and decisions can be made as to what to do next, in order to help individuals or groups of children. Manpreet's June sample of work is very different from her first attempt in the previous October (Example 6). The story of Cinderella is one of her favourites and she wrote her version of the story unaided. The sample shows not only how much Manpreet's writing has developed over the nine month period but also a growth in her use and understanding of English. She can now use complete sentences in English, hold a conversation, retell stories and has started to read independently. Samples of children's work are passed on to their next teacher, along with details about other aspects of their language and literacy development.

Example 6.

> Cinderella went to the ball
> the two ugly sisters s— house
> cinderella d— at the party
> and the king went es the party
> and the king anced with the cinderella.
> And the TM WS MJ NT

Cinderella went to the ball. The two ugly sisters stayed home. Cinderella danced at the party and the king went to the party and the king danced with Cinderella and the time was midnight.

A year in an environment like the one provided by Chris will give all children a good basis for their writing development. Working in this way ensures that children progress at their own speed and level. All attempts are praised and encouragement is given endlessly. Children are relaxed and feel free to have a go at writing. They are confident to display their attempts and to work and share with others. They have become writers.

CHAPTER 11

Drama with Young Learners in School

Joan Anim-Addo

Teachers who are concerned to develop drama with young learners consistently pose a number of questions. At the heart of these is the key question, 'How do I plan for drama to happen in my classroom?' Those who recognise the added richness a multi-ethnic dimension may bring to the learning situation ask also, 'What kind of resources should I be using within drama time in order to best support the group's learning?' This chapter addresses, in the main, the questions above in order to highlight drama as process, with young learners, children aged four to seven.

To illustrate the kind of practice I have in mind, three separate lessons are outlined below. In each of these, the focus is on the children's actions.

Drama observed

What kind of drama can I do with young learners?

The children whose lessons are detailed below are four to six year olds, a multi-ethnic group, inexperienced at drama. Lesson one takes place in the hall; lessons two and three take place in the classroom, a smaller than average space, separated from the rest of the Infant area by a curtain.

Lesson One

The children

– watch the teacher mime a sequence involving stealthy walking, checking over her shoulders, clearing an obstacle away, etc.

- show individually something they have remembered about the mime.
- practise miming the whole sequence.
- respond to the teacher's questions about possible meanings of the mimed actions.
- agree the location, a garden, and in pairs, plan, try out and show a secret meeting in a garden.
- look at large black and white photographs of trees that 'might be special' in such a garden and in twos or threes form these.
- in groups, show the 'magic' trees hiding a person or creature in danger.
- speak the thoughts of the endangered one on a given signal (thought-tracking).

There have been various stops and starts whilst this has been in progress in order to focus the children's thinking and for negotiations between group and teacher. There has been talk about starting positions, speculation about who might be interested to prevent this meeting, the need for secrecy and so on.

Lesson Two

Based in the classroom, the children

- watch a prepared role play (teacher and another), as if overhearing worried sisters afraid to communicate news about a lost sister, Bimwili, to parents.
- question the sisters about their fear (hot seating – that is, sisters in the hot seat).
- in pairs, practise as siblings breaking the worrying news to parents.
- discuss the family's thinking about the lost girl and in groups plan and show a 'frozen picture' of a nightmare about this (still image or tableau).
- as villagers, meet the chief's messenger and answer questions about rumours and fears related to the missing girl (teacher in role).
- in groups, mime what has 'really' happened to Bimwili, having acknowledged the source of the story.
- in groups show a 'frozen picture' of the most frightening moment for her with the Zimwi.
- say, when touched, the thoughts of individual characters (thought-tracking).

Lesson Three

Again based in the classroom, the children

- as picnickers, oversee an unusual bag being retrieved, its contents inspected and sneakily borne away.
- report upon and re-enact this observed sequence, responding to the teacher's challenge for accuracy, she having not 'witnessed' the event.
- speculate about the possible contents of the bag and in pairs take turns being someone interrupted or caught trying to hide the bag while avoiding revealing what is inside to a determined questioner.
- exchange ideas in pairs about who may have lost such an 'important' bag and its possible contents.
- listen and respond to narration informing them of the loss and their own possible implications.

Each lesson evolved from a different resource starting point. Lesson one was related to project work based on the theme 'gardens'. Lesson two developed from interest in a popular picture book, *Bimwili and the Zimwi* (Ardema, 1986) and the third session used an artefact, the bag, as starting point.

These lessons may usefully serve to link three ways in which the teacher could consider supporting the learner in the multi-ethnic classroom. The first way is in achieving some balance in the choice of resource 'literature', for the content of drama sessions. Collections of stories from around the world, such as *The Singing Sack* (East, 1989), are invaluable to this aim, as is a wealth of picture books and poetry anthologies.

A second means is in the significant use of role and supporting resources. Teachers of young children have enviable contact with adults in the child's life. Invitations into school can also service drama purposes, directly, as in the use of person in role (Lawrence, 1982), or indirectly, using information gleaned through an informal talk to the class for the setting up of a role. The use of visual material such as photographs or life size drawings may then be specially supportive of that role. For example, if it is important that a character is a member of a specific ethnic group, then this may be reinforced through documentary material as well as symbolically, such as in the use of a particular item of clothing.

The third and equally important means of support lies in the quality of awareness the teacher utilises in the classroom. At a simple level this may be monitored through noticing which pupil's ideas and opinions are sought and acted upon. A simple observation sheet used to monitor this can sometimes highlight interesting differences between teacher intention and practice.

Examination of the drama sessions, outlined above, reveals the use of a variety of forms which become the early basis of the group's drama. The children have used mime, movement, 'frozen pictures', hot-seating, thought-tracking as well as naturalistic role playing in pairs, groups and the whole group together, with teacher in role. See, for example, Neelands (1990) for detailed information about drama form.

There is, in the drama described, an absence of content regulators such as a script or the following of a known text as in the acting out of a story. What is in operation instead is a crucial structuring of the lesson, through the teacher's knowledge of the dramatic art form, a means offering the teacher vital flexibility. Thus, the focus of the lesson may, as the teacher desires, best serve the intended learning, which, since the group is inexperienced in drama, is as much about drama itself, as about content or social skills. As Neelands (1984) suggests, therein is the 'crux of the learning experience'. For when the child's playing is matched to a range of dramatic forms, a unique educational opportunity emerges.

The teacher of this group, in making the decisions leading to the activities described, draws also upon her knowledge of young children's play. She is requiring the learners to use and develop certain aspects of play, notably their facility at dramatic playing. This she employs in conjunction with knowledge of drama to so structure the lesson as to afford development and allow progression to occur in the selected activities. For drama in education is most concerned with the learning process through which the participant is involved. The questioning, the thinking, the challenging, the adjusting of old knowledge to take account of new situations, the moving to new ways of thinking, the shaping of ideas collaboratively, the engagement of feeling as well as reflection on all of these, are aspects of that process.

Drama as process

What then is the value of drama in the Infant school?

Drama operates within two main strands of cultural behaviour, that of play and more specifically dramatic playing, but also within the conventions of theatre. It is from within the latter that teachers may regularly draw upon techniques and strategies that provide structure for drama lessons. It is from within the former that young learners take on the challenge of those structures and work through the learning possibilities they afford.

Studies of children's behaviour led Vygotsky (1978) to note that play creates 'a zone of proximal development,' a manifestation of which is that children may be observed in play to be behaving above their developmental age. (See Chapter Three for a fuller treatment of this.) An exploration of the child's use of language in such situations may support this.

Not surprisingly then, a significant part of the drama process, for teachers of young learners, is the opportunity it affords for extending the child's already evident competence in spoken language, allowing, as it does, myriad opportunities for exploring and developing ideas, thereby putting thought into speech, and making meaning. An examination of any of the lessons described reveals that the oral skills required of the children included describing, hypothesising, anticipating, explaining, persuading and planning.

Just as in play, where the imaginary situation stimulates an added facility with language, so in drama, it is the imagined dramatic context, a feature of which is immediacy, which acts as a lever to pressurise the participants to response. This response, Bolton (1986) locates within the 'experiencing' end of the drama continuum. It is this area which presents such learning possibilities.

The key to the relationship between play and drama is in the structuring which the teacher employs. It is important to note too that drama presents learners with a way of working which they are predisposed to find attractive. This is a bonus in terms of motivation. Drama looks like play and on a basic level, it is indeed pretend play. With structuring, the teacher has a potent learning medium and one that can readily generate a great deal of enthusiasm.

Part of the appeal of drama is the opportunity it allows for social interaction. The children may have been observed working alternatively in pairs, small groups, and sometimes as a whole large group, with substantial opportunities for social development. It appears then, that within the drama process, several types of learning occur. There is learning about drama itself. There is social learning, since a range of groupings is used; there is content learning and the development of a range of language skills.

Supporting the learner – multi-ethnic realities

There is agreement among drama theorists that drama should relate to the concerns of the children, in terms of ideas for starting and developing drama. This, identified as the 'bite' or motivating force for the children, functions to provide the basic content of the drama, as well as an in-built contract. Any group has a particular interest in developing its own drama, its ideas in action. An important aspect of the teacher's role is, therefore, in gaining the children's ideas and negotiating between differing ideas.

A straightforward means of access to children's thinking is direct enquiry. In groups of thirty, however, this may be impractical. During drama, important thinking may be released. It is useful to develop ways of taking stock of these ideas. A clipboard is useful during and after the session, for recording pertinent observations which may indicate fresh directions for subsequent lessons.

The choices a teacher makes in structuring a drama lesson are related to her knowledge about drama, the group and the area of learning being focussed upon. The result, given the same starting point, could be a variety of lessons. Resources for beginning and developing drama require proper prior thought. A multi-ethnic awareness will require the collecting of documentary resources such as photographs which offer images of different ethnic groups. Often these are difficult to acquire and of indifferent quality. Reproducing them in black and white often adds to their usefulness. The 'bag' lesson for example, was completed without the contents having been revealed to the children. The drama activities served to heighten the significance of the possible content. Another session could build upon this. If, for example *The Valiant Chatti-maker* (Godden, 1983) is to be introduced subsequently into the drama, this could be reflected in the choice of content. This story is also available in dual text, Gujarati and English (Stone, 1988).

The consistent use of material including the literature of any one cultural group, on the basis that the universal implications are clear, does not best serve the needs or interests of all individuals within such a group or indeed of the whole group. A range of narrative material, from a variety of sources, is a basic infinitely flexible resource. Stories are equally valuable resources when drama serves project work. For example, *Bimwili* has a sea-side setting and may service related projects by thoughtful use of resources such as a conch in the drama.

Similar awareness applied to the use of resources such as clothes to be used within the drama repays the time invested. Clothing to depict grandeur may be in a range of material, sari type, cotton with Ashanti stool prints, or plain dyed wool for example. All may be available but the drama is heightened if the symbols are sensitively chosen and used. Similarly, the drama and consequent balance of play may be affected if a fragment of a letter, found in the bottom of the bag, is written in a community language. The valuing of the learner is at issue here and teacher decision-making needs to reflect this. It is also important to appreciate that drama allows for the powerful symbolic use of resources.

Once the drama is set up using appropriate resources, it is critical to utilise the children's ideas. It is a common mistake to believe initially that all ideas for the lesson have to come from the teacher. Rather, ideas from individuals and groups should further the drama or be challenged within the drama. It is after all the group's drama and they will be increasingly motivated to make it theirs as they see their ideas come into play.

Drama and the curriculum

Developing language skills

'Drama is central in developing all major aspects of English in the primary school', states the Cox Report (DES, 1989). In addition, the Statutory Instruments (DES, 1990) have highlighted the role of drama in relation to the early years curriculum principally through the attainment targets for Speaking and Listening.

Speaking and listening

In the absence of transcripts from the lessons already indicated, I offer below an example of a group speaking during a drama session. The extract is taken from drama work with Nursery children, cited in *London Drama* (1990). The drama is based on the picture book, *Ganglehoff* (Murphy, 1986).

> Pupil 1: I've got an idea...
> Pupil 2: He's broken the door down.
> Pupil 3: He's robbed him. He's robbed all the things.
> Pupil 1: Open the gate will you? Quick.
> Teacher: Open the gate! Why? Do you think he's coming again?
> Pupil 1: I've got it. I'll get Batman.

Pupil 4: I don't want to see in there . . . (inaudible) I don't want to see him . . . cause when I see him . . .

Teacher: What will you do to him?

Pupil 4: Kill him.

Teacher: What will you do?

Pupil 4: Kill Ganglehoff.

Teacher: You would kill him if you caught him?

Pupil 5: Yes.

Pupil 6: I would tell my dad. I would tell my dad.

Pupil 3: I would put him in prison.

Teacher: Would you?

Pupil 4: I bang his shirt and throw it in the bin and phone for the police and then put . . . put him in the washing machine. He goes round and round . . .

Teacher: Oh, what would you do, if you could catch him?

Pupil 2: I would put him in prison. I'd tell the police and they might come and take him in prison.

Pupil 6: And when I tell my daddy and we'll punch Ganglehoff.

Noticeably, the children are at different stages in their ability to 'take on' or sustain the dramatic situation. In this episode, children and teacher are in role. This 'being in role' creates an immediacy, which with teacher intervention, propels the 'feeling talk' and actions of the participants.

In the light of concern with the National Curriculum, and particularly its specified attainment targets, the group of four years olds above may be said to be

- responding to a story;
- participating as speakers and listeners in a group engaged in a given task;
- talking with the teacher, listening and answering questions;
- responding to a range of complex instructions given by a teacher;
- relating real or imaginary events in a connected narrative which conveys meaning to a group of pupils, the teacher, or another adult;
- listening with an increased span of concentration to other children and adults, asking and responding to questions and commenting on what has been said.

There are parallels here with the 'Bimwili' lesson, detailed earlier. Both utilise familiar and well loved texts viz. *Ganglehoff* and *Bimwili*. This familiarity with the story operates as a base line, knowledge shared by the whole group. From this collective understanding, further meaning may be explored via aspects of the story undeveloped within the text. Thus, in the 'Bimwili' lesson, the sisters are focal to the teacher's interest in allowing the group opportunity to explore fear.

Other literacy skills

Writing and reading are also recognised as areas which are enhanced through the use of drama. What is less widely appreciated is the extent to which these may be directly linked both to drama and across the whole curriculum.

Writing

Many differing kinds of writing are stimulated by drama work. Writing in a role is a direct response to the drama situation. Perhaps most notable is the place of letter writing in response to a situation which has engaged the feelings as drama does. Drawing-in-role, with captions, also serves a similar function.

The keeping of group or class diaries can also be explored, in addition to shared story writing for the making of individual, group or class books. Building a project based drama can also place the group in a position to discover lack of information material within the school. Individual, group and shared writing can, in such instances, lead to the packaging of factual writing to be used as information material, a resource for the school. For example, in 'Anansi the drummer', from *The Singing Sack*, a feast is featured. An outcome of related written work may be a recipe book of feasts from various parts of the world. Linked to a food project, the drama work becomes central. What much of this writing tends to share is good motivation, clear purpose, and with skilled teacher intervention, a defined audience.

Reading

The reading possibilities created by working through drama are also related to the 'publishing' of such writing. The books may be made available in the library, shared in classrooms or in Assembly and featured in displays. In addition, letters and diary extracts used as 'documents' within the drama, stimulate interest in the written word. The sisters in the 'Bimwili' drama could have alternatively been preparing a note for their parents. Letters are effective, too, when the teacher, in role, cannot read and relies on the group to provide this service.

Across the curriculum

Drama plays a valuable part in enhancing work across the curriculum. Lesson one, referred to earlier, is part of drama work intended to stimulate thinking and further activities in relation to a 'garden' project. Since the drama moves between fantasy and reality, allowing scope for both, a range of related written language activities may arise. As a final activity of the lesson described the group had drawn one item to be found in 'a garden where magic happens'. These drawings were collected on a large sheet to be used as a plan showing a magic garden. From that lesson, map, environmental, or Maths work, exploring scale and size of nearby trees may be explored.

Planning

Teacher questions about planning appear at times to be about 'starting points'. At other times the broader consideration of where the drama is to come from and where it should lead is broached. These questions may be interpreted as referring either to short term planning – involving a series of fairly immediate decisions linked to the structuring of a single drama session – or to a longer term view, encapsulating an awareness of 'what next?'

Planning for drama centres on the teacher task of arriving at useful dramatic activities. There are a variety of routes to this goal as the recommended background reading indicates, since planning is an area of potential growth for all practitioners. When learners are both young and inexperienced, however, the difficulties can appear overwhelming.

The starting point for the planning of a drama session may be a specific stimulus. The 'garden' drama related to topic work but could have been in response to:

- a poem
- a story told
- a book shared
- an artefact

– a natural object
to name only a few possibilities.

The lessons described give strong indication that knowledge about dramatic form is invaluable to planning. Having located, broadly, what the drama is to be about, for example, 'Bimwili', the question of how to work may next be tackled. The class observed were due to work, in their first session, largely in mime, other than when planning, discussing and reflecting. That was the specific teacher's choice for that particular lesson. Even so, other forms have been noted. Invariably, in electing within the range of strategies, possibilities for dramatic action surface. With these listed, and duly considering the intended learning area, a selection may be made of possible activities for the specific group.

Familiarity with the range of strategies is invaluable but choice is determined, in part, by the focus of the lesson. The focus of the 'garden' lesson was about getting used to a secret magical garden. Mime was selected as a strategy for introducing all of that economically. The other activities served to build the group's belief in that garden. The focus of the 'Bimwili' lesson was about being afraid to tell bad news. Unlike the 'garden' drama, the context does not have to be completely invented by the group since it is a story with which they are already familiar. The focus of the 'bag' drama is about the finding of a strange but valuable bag. The teacher however is particularly interested to tap the children's ideas. She uses mime, with which they are becoming familiar, and sets up a hidden object game situation.

The teacher observed had involved each of these stages in planning:

– some initial brain storming, given a topic or starting point
– a determining of the focus of the lesson
– a search for possible strategies or forms to be used
– decisions about grouping the children
– listing of possible dramatic activities for the lesson and selecting from these with a view to developing the lesson in relation to specific learning areas.

Those are a few of the decisive elements which may contribute to the overall lesson plan.

Initially teachers are satisfied to plan for one lesson at a time. It makes sense, also, to consider a longer view of planning such as Heathcote recommends (in Johnson & O'Neill, 1984). There is wisdom in such planning which recognises the value of the resources involved, including teacher time. With this method, the teacher becomes involved in planning for a series of lessons at the outset.

Planning for the 'garden' lesson by this means involves focusing on three main possible areas for dramatic action. Those selected were:

(1) An old/ancient garden (which implies it has a history and therefore allows scope for dramatic inventing).

(2) A powerful new owner has acquired the land. (This allows for the 'wrong' decisions to be made about using the garden and dramatically interesting situations to emerge).

(3) There are plans for the land to be used differently.

With the group, the teacher agrees to utilise all or none of these. They may just be a useful store of dramatic possibilities to be used at decisive points. However, if the drama work is required to be specifically within the boundaries of the selected areas, this can be achieved. For example, if the learning is, for project purposes, to be about a Victorian garden, this will readily impact upon the drama.

Of significance to planning in this way is the search for a single factor which may affect each of the areas outlined and be a source of change, thereby increasing the dramatic tension. The teacher's decisive point of change – that an order has been given for the land to be cleared – makes the possible dramatic action clearer. Thus the garden must first become 'real' to the group and the question of strategies to achieve this becomes paramount.

The plan gives a framework for the drama within the unity of a lesson and can be as flexible as teacher needs dictate. It may indicate also the teacher's role and use of resources. There are various ways of organising groups for drama. In each of the lessons mentioned, the class worked in pairs, larger groups of three or four and sometimes as a whole class working together in a role. This variation in grouping is itself a worthwhile aim. In the process, it offers the teacher the opportunity for observing interactions in differing groups such as the *Primary Language Record* (Barrs, 1988) suggests.

Adequate record keeping provides a substantial contribution to planning, particularly when the teacher takes note of the group's responses – that is, ideas voiced in or out of role during the session. The teacher may be interested to observe a specific group or each group in turn. Within these responses new interests may be identified.

Reflection

It is within opportunities for reflection that the teacher can readily gauge learning taking place. This may happen in discussion between activities, though it is also useful to consider including in the planning, ways of working in role which are essentially times for group reflection. 'Frozen' pictures and thought-tracking can, for example, be used to aid reflection. Changing the teacher role is another useful means of assisting reflection. For example, in the 'Ganglehoff' episode, the teacher had switched role from frightened neighbour to reporter, thus allowing a different opportunity for re-assessing behaviour and attitudes.

Moving into role

Dorothy Heathcote (in Johnson and O'Neill, 1984) gives role taking as a broad definition of educational drama. While thought needs to be given to teacher role, particularly in relation to status implied in those roles, careful thought needs to be given to the kinds of role young children are asked to undertake. It makes for greater clarity on the learner's part if these are task related. For example, to be asked to be a villager is not sufficiently informative considering how far removed this may be from the experience of the average urban five year old. But to be a villager preparing for a party gives the young person more upon which to draw. This is not to ascribe unwarranted limitations to young learners whose flexibility, awareness and experience are not to be underestimated. It is really a plea about making the objectives of lessons as accessible to many as possible. It is also about being aware enough to so balance the demands made upon the learners as to be challenging whilst building upon what the children already know.

The use of drama in the classroom contributes considerably to 'good' practice. Within this there is the real teacher task of understanding 'the nature, texture and power of the action we set up for our pupils.' (O'Neill, 1988). A result of this is increasing confidence in approaching the raw material of ideas and themes, and extracting more precisely what is needed for the drama lesson.

PART FOUR:

Resources

Resources

Some criteria for the choice of suitable resources (books, videos, packs, etc.) for young children

(1) We live in a multi-ethnic, multi-cultural society. Recently produced material which ignores this fact should only be used if there is no substitute for it.

(2) Material presented to children below Junior school age should not need to have too much contextualising in order to make its content acceptable and 'non-racist'. (Older children may gain a good deal from examining outdated material in order to understand why the attitudes in it are unacceptable).

(3) Nothing presented as 'anti-racist' or 'multi-cultural' should be below the standard of writing or production which is normally demanded in any other materials given to children.

(4) Any kind of stereotyping which leads to bias should be avoided (race, sex, class, negatively presented species of animals, etc.). The fact that a book or video is an effective piece of anti-racism does not justify it being sexist, for instance! Also, while animal stereotypes such as the 'big bad wolf' cannot be entirely avoided, try to select some stories which present wolves, foxes, rats, spiders, etc. in a positive light!

(5) The diet should be varied: fact/fiction; fantasy/realistic; British/abroad; boys/girls or preferably mixed groups of children; black/white/Asian, as leading characters etc.

(6) Racist terms should be avoided in material for young children, even if they are only being used to show what is wrong with them!

(7) No child should be made to feel embarrassed or inferior because of any material which is used.

(8) Opportunities to bring out positive messages about people of different origins should be used, but not in any heavily didactic way.

(9) Where possible, opportunities should exist in which both the similarities and the differences between people of various races and cultures can be presented. The aim is to interest and inform, but *never* to make the children think, 'These people are funny!'

(10) The objective is to help children make their own choices and judgements, rather than to make decisions for them.

Guides to selection of books and resources

Adler, S. (n.d.) *Equality Street: A Penguin Multi-Cultural Booklist.* Harmondsworth: Penguin.

The *Books for Keeps* Guide to *Children's Books for a Multi-Cultural Society, 0–7* and *8–12* (1986). Compiled by Judith Elkin, Edited by Pat Triggs. *Books for Keeps*, 6 Brightfield Rd., Lee, London SE12 8QF. Tel: 081 852 4953.

The Dual Language Collection 1990: Roy Yates Books, 40 Woodfield Rd., Rudgwick, Horsham, West Sussex, RH12 3EP.

The Good Book Guide to Children's Books (1983). Harmondsworth: Penguin.

The New Current Awareness List for Asian and Afro-Caribbean Poetry, produced by The Poetry Library, Royal Festival Hall, London, SE1 8XX.

Stories in the Multilingual Primary Classroom: Supporting Children's Learning of English as a Second Language (Centre for Urban Educational Studies, 1983).

Stones, R. (n.d.) *A Penguin Multi-Ethnic Booklist.* London: Penguin.

Tamarind: Education through Involvement (Books, Puzzles, other learning materials), Tamarind Educational Products, P.O. Box 296, Camberley, Surrey, GU15 1QW. Tel: 0276 683979.

Centres, Associations etc.

ACER Afro-Caribbean Education Resource Centre, Wyvil School, Wyvil Rd., London SW8 2TJ. Tel: 071 627 2662.

ACERT Advisory Council for Education of Romany and other Travellers, Moot House, The Stow, Harlow, Essex, CM20 3AG.

AIMER Access to Information on Multicultural Educational Resources, Bulmershe College, Woodlands Ave, Reading RG6 1HY.

ALIRT Association for Literacy Teaching and Research, c/o Liz Grugeon, Bedford College of Higher Education, Polhill Ave., Bedford, MK41 9E.

Building Blocks, 40 Tabard Street, London SE1 4JU. (Resources for use in training teachers or carers). Tel: 071 403 8264.

Centre for Language in Primary Education, Webber Row, London SE1 8WQ. Tel: 071 633 0840.

Centre for Urban Education (CUES) Lilian Baylis School, Lawn Lane, London, SW8. Tel: 071 735 0656.

Children's Book Foundation, Book Trust, Book House, 45 East Hill, London SW18 2QZ. Tel: 081 870 9055.

Commission for Racial Equality, Elliott House, 10–12 Allington St., London SW1.

Development Education Centre, Gillett Centre, Selly Oak College, Bristol Rd., Birmingham.

The Letterbox Library, 1st Floor, 5 Bradbury St., London N16 8JN. Tel: 071 254 1640.

Multi-Link – an integrated multi-cultural service. 7 Greenhill, Wembley, Middx. HA9 9BR. Tel: 081 446 9422.

National Association for the Teaching of English, c/o Birley High School, Fox Lane, Frenchville, Sheffield, S12 4WY.

National Association for Multiracial Education.

National Association for Teachers of Travellers, Fenby Base, Lorne St., Wakefield Rd. Bradford, BD4 7PS.

United Kingdom Reading Association, c/o Edge Hill College, St. Helen's Rd. Ormskirk, Lancs.

The Working Group Against Racism in Children's Resources, 460 Wandsworth Rd., London SW8 3LX.

Journals

Bookbird, Mayerhofgasse 6 A1040 Vienna Austria.

Books for Keeps, 6 Brightfield Rd., Lee, London SE12 8QF.

Dragon's Teeth, National Committee on Racism in Children's Books, 5 Cornwall Crescent, Basement Office, London W11 1PH.

Education Impact, Box 905 Marlow, Buckinghamshire, SL7 2UA.

Journal of Multicultural Librarianship, 95 Hopton Rd., London SW16 2EL.

Junior Education, c/o Scholastic Publications Ltd., Marlborough House, Holly Walk, Leamington Spa, Warwicks, CV32 4LS.

Language in Education, Language Matters, Centre for Language in Primary Education, 9 Webber Row, London SE1 8QW.

Multicultural Teaching, Trentham Books, 30 Wenger Crescent, Trentham, Stoke on Trent, ST4 8LE.

NATE News, c/o Birley High School, Fox Lane, Frenchville, Sheffield, S12 4WY.

The North Circular, The Magazine of the North London Language Consortium.

T.A.L.K., Journal of the National Oracy Project, Newcombe House, 45 Notting Hill Gate, London W11 3JB. Tel: 071 229 1234.

The School Librarian, The School Library Association, Liden Library, Barrington Close, Liden, Swindon, SN3 6HF.

WGARCR Newsletters, published by Working Group Against Racism in Children's Resources, 460 Wandsworth Rd., London SW8 3LX.

Audio visual material

By Word of Mouth (A four part series from Channel Four on storytelling, with booklet) Broadside Publications, 17B Finsbury Park Rd., London N4 2LA.

Educating the Whole Child (Video with supporting material), Building Blocks, 40 Tabard St., London SE1 4JU.

Eye of the Storm, Getting to Grips with Racism, A Class Divided (Three videos from BBC Enterprises, Wood Lane, London W12 0TI).

Mosaic (Six part training series, including investigation of Nursery school provision and the needs of bilingual children). Room 403, London W5 2PA. Tel: 081 670 0394.

To School Together (Video discussing parental concerns) ACER, Wyvil School, Wyvil Rd., London SW8.

Packs

Chan, M., Lawton, J., Town, A., Carter, R. (ed. Sallnow, A.) (1990) *Fruit Project Pack*. London: Mantra.

North London Language Consortium (NLLC) *Guidelines for Using . . . North London Planning and Assessment Framework*. London: NLLC.

Schools Examination and Assessment Council (S.E.A.C.) (n.d.) *A Guide to Teacher Assessment*, Packs, A, B & C. London: Heinemann.

S.E.A.C. (1991) *School Assessment Folder: Key Stage One*. London: H.M.S.O.

Some books of multi-cultural interest

(Note that many of these books have been published in paperback subsequent to first publication).

Picture books including characters from ethnic minority groups

(In many instances these characters are incidental, and their identities may only be deduced from the illustrations).

Aardema, V. (1981) (illus. Beatriz Vidal) *Bringing the Rain to Kapiti Plain*. African folk-tale. London: Macmillan.

Aardema, V. (1985) (illus. Marc Brown) *Oh Kojo how could you?* An Ashanti tale. London: Hamish Hamilton.

Agard, J. (1981) *Dig Away Two Hole Tim*. A dialect story set in the Caribbean. London: Bodley Head.

Agard, J. (1990) *Go Noah Go*. London: Hodder & Stoughton. The story of a West Indian Noah and his wife, in dialect rhyme.

Agard, J. (illus. Jennifer Bent) (1990) *The Calypso Alphabet*. London: Collins.

Ahlberg J. & A., (1982) *The Baby's Catalogue*. Harmondsworth: Penguin.

Ahlberg, J. & A., (1988) *Starting School*. Harmondsworth: Penguin.

Amery, H. & Cartwright, S. (1987) *The First Hundred Words*. London: Usborne.

Aniego, J. & Dewey, A. (1990) *Rock a Bye Crocodile*. Fantasy in a foreign setting. London: Walker Books.

Appiah, S. (illus. Carol Easmon) (1989) *Amoko & Efua Bear*. African setting for story of lost teddy bear. London: Andre Deutsch.

Blackman, M. (illus. Rhian Nest Jones) (1991) *That New Dress*. A child wants a new dress which she sees in a shop, but her mother makes one instead, to her immediate chagrin but eventual triumph. New York: Simon & Schuster.

Bodsworth, N. (1989) *A Nice Walk in the Jungle*. Story of a multi-racial class with a forgetful teacher. When she at last notices that all her class have been eaten by a boa constrictor, she easily defeats it. Harmondsworth: Penguin.

Bonnici, P. (illus. Lisa Kopper) (1985) *Amber's Other Grandparents*. Child of mixed race meets grandparents from India. London: Bodley Head.

Bradman, T. & Browne, E. (1990) *In a Minute*. London: Methuen.

Bradman, T. & Browne, E. (1988) *Wait and See*. London: Methuen.

The above three books all portray a family with a black mother and a white father.

Brennan, M. (1986) *Denise and Louise*. Story of two black sisters, an old man and a dog. Illus. by real photos. London: Peckham Publishing Project, 13 Peckham High St., SE15.

Brienburg, P. (illus. Errol Lloyd) (1973) *My Brother Sean*. A child who wants to go to school but doesn't like it when he gets there. London: Bodley Head.

Caines, J. (illus. Pat Cummings) (1984, text 1982) *Just Us Women*. Child spends the day with her aunt. New York: Harper & Row.

Davies, A. & D. (illus. Paul Dowling) (1990) *Poonam's Pets*. A shy girl brings six enormous lions to school – no awkward questions about probability are asked. London: Methuen.

Elliott, O. (illus. Amanda Welch) (1989) *Under Sammy's Bed*. London: Andre Deutsch.

Elliott, O. (illus. Amanda Welch) (1990) *Sammy goes Flying*. London: Andre Deutsch.

Flournoy, V. (illus. Jerry Pinkney) (1985) *The Patchwork Quilt*. Child and grandmother: each piece of patchwork brings memories and complex emotions. London: Bodley Head.

French, F. (1971) *Halni*. Good treatment of Egyptian myth. Oxford: University Press.

Gandhi, N. (illus. Amanda Welch) (1990) *Sari Games*. London: Andre Deutsch.

Ganley, H. (1986) *Jyoti's Journey*. The journey is from a village in India. London: Andre Deutsch.

Gibbons, A. (illus. Toni Goffe) (1990) *Our Peculiar Neighbour*. A multiracial group of children have a vampire as a neighbour. London: Dent.

Godden, R. (1983) *The Valient Chatti Maker*. London: Macmillan.

Greenfield, E. (illus. Floyd Cooper) (1988) *Grandpa's Face*. Child is frightened when Grandpa looks cross but he is only acting. London: Hutchinson.

Grindley, S. (illus. Jo Burroughs) (1990) *Meet the Family*. London: Orchard.

Havill, J. (illus. A. Sibley O'Brien) (1990) *Jamaica Tag Along*. Also includes anti-sexist motif – a little girl is rejected because the boys want to play football; she eventually lets a little boy share her game *and* builds such a good castle that the older boys envy her. London: Heinemann.

Havill, J. (illus. A. Sibley O'Brien) (1990) *Jamaica's Find*. London: Mandarin.

Hearn, E. (illus. Mark Thurman) (1984) *Good Morning Frances good night Frances*. Features a black girl in a wheel chair who plays in the park. Toronto: Women's Press.

Hoffman, M. & Northway, J. (1990) *Nancy No-Size*. A child is eventually old and big enough to go to school. London: Mandarin.

Hughes, S. (1988) *The Big Alfie and Annie Rose Story Book*. Hughes' books, often set in Trotter Street, always include characters from a range of different ethnic backgrounds. London: Bodley Head.

Impey, R. & Porter, S. (1986) *Tough Teddy*. (But he isn't that tough really!) London: Heinemann.

Keats, E. J. (1966) *Whistle for Willie*. London: Bodley Head.

Keats, E. J. (1968) *Peter's Chair*. London: Bodley Head.

Keats, E. J. (1970) *Goggles*. London: Bodley Head

(All these books by E. J. Keats are concerned with family relationships).

Keeping, C. (1967) *Charley Charlotte and the Golden Canary*. Friendship between white and black children shown in pictures but race not explicitly in text. Oxford: University Press.

Lloyd, E. (1978) *Nini at Carnival*. Her fairygodmother makes Nini the queen of the carnival. London: Bodley Head.

Lloyd, E. (1990) *Ravi at the Funfair*. London: Blackie, 1990.

Lloyd, E. (1989) *Y has a long tail*. Lenny asks lots of questions. London: Blackie.

MacDonald, I. (illus. Rhian Nest Jones) (1991) *Khuumalo's Market*. An African tale. New York: Simon & Schuster.

May, K. (illus. Doffy Weir) (1989) *Knickerless Nicola*. Title character has a black neighbour. London: Macmillan.

Mitra, M. (1986) *My First Railway Journey*. No text, pictures self explanatory. India: National Book Trust.

Morgan, M. & Porter, S. (1990) *The Monster is Coming*. Edinburgh: Canongate.

Morris, A. (1989) *Uzman's Photo Album*. Very factual about the Punjab. London: A. & C. Black.

Murphy, B. (1986) *Ganglehoff*. Harmondsworth: Penguin.

Northway, J. (1991) *Lucy's Day Trip*. Black girl with white father and cousin. London: Andre Deutsch.

Oakley, J. (1989) *Would You be Angry?* Varied range of children: not so much a story as a range of situations for possible discussion. London: Andre Deutsch.

Owen, G. (illus. Bob Wilson) (1990) *Ruby and the Dragon*. A black girl who because of her costume in a play succeeds in scaring the men who are robbing the school. London: Collins.

Padmanabhan, M. (1986) *A Visit to the City Market*. No text, pictures self explanatory. India: The National Book Trust.

Pearce, P. (illus. Helen Ganly) (1987) *The Tooth Ball*. Timmy is befriended by black boy living opposite. London: Andre Deutsch.

Pirotta, S. (illus. Mrinal Mitra) (1990) *Do you Believe in Magic?* London: Dent.

Pirotta, S. & Cooper, H. (1989) *Solomon's Secret*. A black child from London is transported into a fantasy environment. London: Methuen.

Pitts Walter, M. (illus. Pat Cummings) (1990) *Little Sister, Big Trouble*. More of an illustrated story than a picture book. Illustrations indicate Caribbean origin. New York: Simon & Schuster.

Pooley, S. & Chappell, A. (1990) *An Outing for Oliver*. London: Blackie.

Ramachandran, A. (1979) *Hanuman*. Traditional story quite well told, illustrations non-realistic. London: A. & C. Black.

Richardson, J. & Carey, J. (1989) *A Dog for Ben*. Harmondsworth: Penguin.

Samuels, V. (illus. Jennifer Northway) (1989) *Boxed In*. A little boy, accidentally shut in a cupboard, imagines he won't be found for a long while, but in fact is found soon. London: Bodley Head.

Schermbrucker, R. (illus. Niki Daly) (1989) *Charlie's House*. Set in a shanty town in South Africa. London: Walker Books.

Seeger, P. (1986) *Abiyoyo*. London: Hamish Hamilton.

Smith, M. (illus. Lesley Moyes) (1990) *Annie and Moon*. Story about a girl and a cat. Harmondsworth: Penguin.

Snape, J. & C. (1984) *Daniel likes Dancing*. Non-sexist as well as non-racist. London: Julia MacRae.

Thomas, I. (illus. Jennifer Northway) (1990) *Princess Janine*. Child goes to a Safari Park. London: Andre Deutsch.

Thomas, I. (illus. J. Northway) (1987) *Janine and the Carnival*. Child gets lost, which provides the opportunity for lots of pictures of the carnival. London: Andre Deutsch.

Thomson, R. & N. (1988) *Whatever Next? – A Story Set in Trinidad*. Illus. with photographs. London: A. & C. Black.

Wade, B. (illus. Katinka Kew) (1990) *Little Monster*. Mandy behaves badly but consolidates her understanding that she is loved in spite of this. London: Andre Deutsch.

Wilkins, V. (1987) *Mom Can Fix It*. Camberley: Tamarind.

Wilkins, V. (1987) *Ben makes a cake*. Camberley: Tamarind.

(These two books incidentally challenge sexist stereotyping).

Collections of poetry and folk tales

Agard, J. (1983) *I Din Do Nuttin*. London: Bodley Head.

Agard, J. (1990) *Laughter is an Egg*. Harmondsworth: Penguin.

Agard, J. (1987) *Lend me Your Wings*. London: Hodder & Stoughton.

Agard, J. (1986) *Say It Again Granny: Twenty Poems from Caribbean Proverbs*. London: Bodley Head.

Agard, J. & Nichols, G. (1991) *No Hickory No Dickory No Dock: A Collection of Caribbean Nursery Rhymes*. Harmondsworth: Penguin.

Carlstrom, N. (1987) *Wild Wild Sunflower Child Anna*. London: Macmillan.

Cook, H. & Styles, M. (1991) (eds.) *Catch them if you can*. Cambridge: University Press.

Craft, R. (1988) *The Day of the Rainbow*. London: Heinemann.

East, H. (1989) *The Singing Sack*. London: A. & C. Black.

Foster, J. (1985) (ed.) *A Very First Poetry Book*. Oxford: University Press.

Foster, J. (1991) (ed.) *Another First Poetry Book*. Oxford: University Press.

Hudson, C. W. & Ford, B. G. (1990) *Bright Eyes Black Skin*. Orange, New Jersey: Just Us Books.

Ijoma, W. (1978) *A Child's Book of African Poetry*. London: Macmillan.

Kerven, R. (1991) *Earth Magic, Sky Magic: North American Indian Tales*. Cambridge: University Press.

Lloyd, E. (1989) *I Don't Care*. London: Blackie.

Marzolla, J. & Pinkney, J. (1990) *What Else Can You Do?* London: Bodley Head.

Nichols, G. (1988) *Come into My Tropical Garden*. London: A. & C. Black.

Oxenbury, H. (1987) *Clap Hands*. London: Walker Books.

Pitcher, D. (illus. Meg Rutherford) (1980) *The Calabash Child*; *African Folk Tales Adapted and Retold*. Cape Town: David Philip.

Simeon, K. & Stewart, S. (1989) *The Streetwise Kid*. London: Blackie

Stones, R. & Mann, A. (1977) *Mother Goose Comes to Cable Street*. Harmondsworth: Penguin.

Tadjo, V. (1988) *Lord of the Dance; An African Retelling*. London: A. & C. Black.

Williams, J. (1987) *Ride a Cock Horse: Animal Rhymes*. Harmondsworth: Penguin.

Animal books which can be used in an anti-racist way

Aardema, V. (1977) *Who's in Rabbit's House?* London: Bodley Head.

Aardema, V. (1986) *Bimwili and the Zimwi*. London: Hamish Hamilton.

Burningham, J. (1970) *Mr. Gumpy's Outing*. London: Jonathan Cape.

Carle, E. (1977) *The Bad Tempered Ladybird*. London: Hamish Hamilton.

Kerr, J. (1968) *The Tiger who came to Tea*. London: Collins.

McKee, D. (1989) *Elmer*. Book about a patchwork elephant, particularly suggesting the value of differences. London: Hutchinson.

McKee, D. (1978) *Tusk Tusk*. Black and white elephants fight, and the only survivors, who run away, give rise to grey elephants. London: Andersen.

Rosen, M. (1987) *We're Going on a Bear Hunt*. London: Walker Books.
Seeger, P. (1987) *Abiyoyo*. London: Hamish Hamilton.
Smyth, G. & James, A. (1989) *A Pet for Mrs. Arbuckle*. Harmondsworth: Penguin.

Books with more text

Ashley, B. (1981) *I'm trying to tell you*. London: Viking.
Aldred, M. (19857 *Marcana the Fairy*. London: Karmah House, 300 Westbourne Rd., W11 1EH. 4 stories, one showing that there can be black fairies.
Bond, R. (1989) *Ghost Trouble*. London: Julia MacRae.
Breinburg, P. (1980) *Brinsley's Dream*. Harmondsworth: Penguin.
Cameron, A. (1982) *The Julian Stories*. London: Gollancz. There are several other volumes about this ingenious Caribbean boy.
Cate, D. (illus. Beryl Sanders) (1990) *Ben's Big Day*. New York: Simon & Schuster.
Dharmi, N. (1990) *A Medal for Malvin*. London: Antelope.
Edwards, D. (1971) *Joe and Timothy Together*. Harmondsworth: Penguin.
Escott, J. (1989) *Wayne's Luck*. London: Blackie.
French, V. (1990) *Zenobia and Mouse*. London: Walker Books.
Gavin, J. (1983) *Kamla and Kate*. London: Methuen.
Gavin, J. (1990) *I want to be an Angel*. London: Methuen.
Gavin, J. (1991) *Kamla and Kate Again*. London: Methuen.
Hallworth, G. (1984) *Tales from the West Indies, Mouth Open Story Jump Out*. London: Methuen.
Hill, E. S. (illus. Sandra Speidel) (1991) *Evan's Corner*. London: Viking. New issue of story first published in 1967.
Hoffman, M. (ed.) (1990) *Ip Dip Sky Blue*. London: Collins.
Joy. M. (1985) *Allotment Lane School*. Harmondsworth: Penguin.
Kaye, G. (1989) *Summer in Small Street*. London: Methuen.
Kaye, G. (1990) *Winter in Small Street*. London: Methuen.
Kaye, G. (1963) *Kofi and the Eagle*. London: Methuen.
Kaye, G. (1980) *The Beautiful Take Away Palace*. London: Kaye & Ward.
Medlicott, M. (1990) *Time for Telling*. London: Kingfisher.
Newman, M. (1990) *Green Monster Magic*. London: Corgi.
Sampson, F. (1985) *Chris and the Dragon*. London: Gollancz.
Smith, N. (illus. Barbara Walker) (1987) *Will you Come on Wednesday*? London: Walker Books.
Smith, N. (illus. Rhian Nest Jones) (1990) *Imran's Secret*. London: Julia MacRae.
Smith, A. M. (1990) *The Ice-Cream Bicycle*. Harmondsworth: Penguin.
Steptoe, J. (1987) *Mufao's Beautiful Daughters*. London: Hamish Hamilton.
Walsh, J. P. (illus. Jennifer Northway) (1982) *Babylon*. London: Andre Deutsch.
Wilkins, V. (1988) *Mike and Lottie*. Camberley: Tamarind.

Bibliography

Acton, T. & Kenrick, D. (1984) *Romani Rockkeripen. To-divvus*, London: Romanestan publications, Thames Polytechnic.

Anim-Addo, J. (1990) 'Moving from Story to Drama with Nursery Children', in *London Drama*, March 1990.

Arnberg, L. (1987) *Raising Children Bilingually: the Pre-school Years*. Clevedon: Multilingual Matters.

All London Teachers Against Racism and Fascism (ALTARF) (1984) *Challenging Racism*. London: ALTARF.

Alladina, S. & Edwards, V. (1990) (eds.) *Multilingualism in the British Isles*, vols. I & II. London: Longmans.

Aunins, A. (1990) *Multicultural Play*. Nottingham: Nottingham Educational Supplies.

Bain, B. *et al*. (1991) 'Drama the Perfect Lure', in *The Drama Magazine*, March 1991.

Baker, C. (1988) *Key Issues in Bilingualism and Bilingual Education*. Clevedon: Multilingual Matters Ltd.

Barnes, D. (1976) *From Communication to Curriculum*. Harmondsworth: Penguin Books.

Barnes, D., Britton, J. & Rosen, H. (1969) *Language, the Learner and the School*. Harmondsworth: Penguin.

Barrs, M. 'Voice and Role in Reading and Writing', in *London Drama*, vol. 7, no. 6.

Barrs, M. *et al*. (1989) *The Primary Language Record*. London: Inner London Education Authority.

Barrs, M., Ellis, S., Hester, H. & Thomas, A. (1990) *Patterns of Learning*. London: Centre for Language in Primary Education.

Bee, H. (1981) (2nd editn) *The Developing Child*. London: Harper & Row.

Ben-Zeev, S. (1977) 'Mechanisms by which childhood bilingualism affects understanding of language and cognitive structures', in Hornby, P. A., (1977) (ed.) *Bilingualism: Psychological, Social and Educational Implications*. New York: Academic Press.

Bernstein, B. (1970) 'Education cannot compensate for society', in *New Society*, 26th Feb., 1970, pp. 344–7.

Bernstein, B. (1974) 'A Critique of the Concept of Compensatory Education' in (ed.) Wedderburn, D. *Poverty, Inequality and Class Structure*. Cambridge: University Press.

Berry, K. (1990) 'In my view', in *Child Education*, January 1990.

Bettelheim, B. (1976) *The Uses of Enchantment: the Meaning and Importance of Fairy Tales*. London: Thames and Hudson.

Bolton, G. (1984) *Drama as Education*. London: Longmans.

Bolton, G. (1986) *Selected Writings*. London: Longmans.

Brown, D. (1979) *Mother Tongue to English: The Young Child in the Multicultural School*. Cambridge: University Press.

Bruner, J. (1986) *Actual Minds, Possible Worlds*. Cambridge, Mass.: Harvard University Press.

Bryant, P. & Bradley, L. (1985) *Children's Reading Problems*. Oxford: Blackwell.

Carrington, B. & Short, G. (1989) *'Race' and the Primary School*. Windsor: NFER-Nelson.

Catalogue of Languages Spoken by ILEA Pupils. (1987) London: Inner London Education Authority.

Cheshire, J. (1982a) *Variation in an English Dialect*. Cambridge: University Press.

Cheshire, J. (1982b) 'Dialect Features and Linguistic Conflict in Schools', in *Educational Review*, Vol. 34, No. 1.

Chivers, T. S. (1987) *Race and Culture in Education: Issues arising from the Swann Report*. Windsor: NFER-Nelson.

Clark, M. M. (1976) *Young Fluent Readers*. London: Heinemann Education.

Clay, M. (1975) *What did I Write?* London: Heinemann.

Cohen, L. & Manion, L. (1983) *Multicultural Classrooms*. Beckenham: Croom Helm.

Colwell, E. (1991) *Storytelling*. Stroud: Thimble Press.

Commission for Racial Equality (1988) *Learning in Terror: A Survey of Racial Harassment in Schools and Colleges*. London: CRE.

Cox, C. B. (1989) *English for Ages 5-16*. London: H.M.S.O.

Craft, M. (1984) *Education and Cultural Pluralism*. Lewes: Falmer.

Cummins, J. & Swain, M. (1986) *Bilingualism in Education*. London: Longmans.

D.E.S. (1988) *National Curriculum Task Group on Assessment and Testing: Three Supplementary Reports*. London: H.M.S.O.

D.E.S. (1989) *Drama from 5-16*. (H.M.I. Curriculum Matters 17) London: H.M.S.O.

D.E.S. (1990) *English in the National Curriculum*. London: H.M.S.O.

D.E.S. (1990) *National Curriculum Assessment Arrangements*. London: H.M.S.O.

D.E.S. (1990) *The Teaching and Learning of Drama*. London: H.M.S.O.

Dickinson, P. (1970) 'A Defence of Rubbish', in Fox, G. *et al.* (1976) (eds.) *Writers, Critics and Children*. London: Heinemann.

Dixon, B. (1977) *Catching them Young: Volume I, Sex, Race and Class in Children's Fiction*. London: Pluto.

Dixon, B. (1982) *Now Read On: Recommended Fiction for Young People*. London: Pluto.

Dudley, P. (1991) 'Word Blind Legislation', *Times Educational Supplement*, 19th April, 1991.

Edwards, J. R. (1979) *Language and Disadvantage*. London: Arnold.

Edwards, V. (1979) *The West Indian Language in British Schools*. London: Routledge.

Edwards, V. (1983) *Language in Multi-Cultural Classrooms*. London: Batsford.

Edwards, V. (1986) *Language in a Black Community*. Clevedon: Multilingual Matters.

Edwards, V., Goodwin, J. & Wellings, A. (1991) *English 7-14: Every Child's Entitlement*. London: David Fulton.

Ehri, L. C. (1979) 'Linguistic Insight: Threshold of Reading Acquisition', in Waller, T. G. & Mackinnon, G. E. (1979) *Reading Research in Theory and Practice*. New York.

Emblen, V. & Schmitz, H. (1991) *Learning Through Story*. Leamington Spa: Scholastic (Bright Ideas Series).

Fantini, A. (1985) *Language Acquisition of a Bilingual Child: A Sociolinguistic Perspective*. Clevedon: Multilingual Matters.

Farrell, P. (1991) *Multicultural Education*. Leamington Spa: Scholastic.

Ferdman, B. M. 'Literacy and Cultural Identity', *Harvard Education Review*, Vol. 60, No. 2, pp. 181–204.

Frederickson, N. & Cline, T. (eds.) (1990) *Curriculum Related Assessment with Bilingual Children (A Set of Working Papers)*. London: University College.

Freire, P. (1967) *Education as the Price of Freedom*. Rio de Janiero: Paz e Terra.

Garrett, R. (1991) *Does Story Telling Affect the Literacy Development of Young Children*? Unpublished B.Ed. In-Service Dissertation, London: Thames Polytechnic.

Garvey, E. (1990) *Story as Vehicle: Teaching English to Young Children*. Clevedon: Multilingual Matters Ltd.

Gersie, A. & King, N. (1990) *Storymaking in Education and Therapy*. London: Jessica Kingsley Publishers.

Gersie, A. (1991) *Storymaking in Bereavement: Dragons Fight in the Meadow*. London: Jessica Kingsley Publishers.

Goodman, Y. M. & Burke, C. L. (1972) *Reading Miscue Inventory Manual*. London: Macmillan.

Gravelle, M. (1990) 'Assessment and Bilingual Pupils', in *Multicultural Teaching*, 9.1.

Gregory, A. & Woolland, N. (1985) (eds.) *Looking into Language Diversity in the Classroom*. Stoke on Trent: Trentham Books.

Grosjean, F. (1982) *Life with two languages; an Introduction to Bilingualism*. Harvard: University Press.

Heller, M. (1987) 'The Role of Language in the Formation of Ethnic Identity', in Phinney J. S. & Rotheran, M. J. (1987) *Children's Ethnic Socialisation: Pluralism and Development*. Newbury Park CA: Sage.

Hewitt, R. (1986) *White Talk, Black Talk*. Cambridge: University Press.

Hicks, D. W. (1981) *Minorities: a Teacher's Resource Book for the Multi-ethnic curriculum*. London: Heinemann.

Hornby, P. A. (1977) (ed.) *Bilingualism: Psychological, Social and Educational Implications*. New York: Academic Press.

Houlton, D. (1985) *All our Languages*. London: Edward Arnold.

Hounslow Language Service: Primary Team (1991) *Assessment and Record Keeping for Bilingual Pupils*. Hounslow: Language Service.

Hughes, M. (1990) 'Parents and the National Curriculum', in *Early Years Paper 2*. London: Thames Polytechnic. More details of Sonnyboy are in Cousins, J. 'Are your Little Humpty Dumpties Floating or Sinking?', *Early Years*, vol. 10, pp. 28–38, and in Hughes, M. & Cousins, J. 'The Roots of Oracy: Early Language at Home and School', in MacLure, M. *et al.* (eds.) (1988) *Oracy Matters: The Development of Talking and Listening in Education*. Milton Keynes: Open University Press.

Hughes, T. 'Myth and Education', in Fox, G. *et al.* (1976) (eds.) *Writers, Critics and Children*. London: Heinemann. Also in Egan, K. & Nadaner, D. (eds.) (1988) *Imagination and Education*. Milton Keynes: Open University Press.

James, A. & Jeffcoate, R. (1981) (eds.) *The School in the Multicultural Society*. London: Harper & Row.

Jeffcoate, R. (1986) *Ethnic Minorities and Education*. London: Harper & Row.

Johnson, K. (1991) *Has Storytelling a Place in Education*? Unpublished B.Ed. Primary English Special Study. London: Thames Polytechnic.

Johnson, L. & O'Neill, C. (1984) *Dorothy Heathcote: Collected Writings on Education and Drama*. London: Hutchinson.

Jones, P. (1988) *Lip Service: the Story of Talk in Schools*. Milton Keynes: Open University.

Jupp, C. *et al.* (1988/9) *Bilingual Support Project*. Hounslow: Language Service: Primary Team.

Kenrick, D. & Puxon, G. (1972) *The Destiny of Europe's Gipsies*. London: Chatto.

Klein, G. (1985) *Reading Into Racism: Bias in Children's Literature and Learning Materials*. London: Routledge.

Labov, W. (1969) 'The logic of non-standard English', in Giglioli, P. (ed.) *Language and Social Context*. Harmondsworth: Penguin.

Lawrence, C. (1982) 'Teacher and Role', in *2D*, Spring 1982, vol. 12.

Lawton, J. (1990) *English in the National Curriculum: Implications for Bilingual Learners*. Hounslow: Language Service: Primary Team, Newsletters.

Lee, N. (1978) *Gavverred All Around*. Manchester: Traveller Education Service.

Leeson, R. (1985) *Reading and Righting*. London: Collins.

Leith, D. (1983) *A Social History of English*. London: Routledge.

Librarians Anti-Racist Strategies Group (n.d.) *Criteria for the Assessment of Literature and Learning Resources for Young People*. London: Working Group Against Racism in Children's Resources.

Liegeois, J. P. (1986) *Gipsies, An Illustrated History*, London: All Sagi books.

MacNamara, J. (1979) 'What Happens to Children whose Home Language is not that of the School?', in Verma, G. & Bagley, C. (1979) *Race, Education and Identity*. London: Macmillan.

Mayor, B. (1988) 'What it Means to be Bi-Lingual' in Mercer, N. (1988) (ed.) *Language and Literacy*. Vol. 1. Milton Keynes: Open University.

Mead, M. (1971) in Tanner, J. M. & Inhelder, B. (eds.) *Discussion on Child Development*. London: Tavistock Publications.

Meek, M. (1988) *How Texts Teach What Readers Learn*. Stroud: Thimble Press.

Meek, M. (1991) *On Being Literate*. London: Bodley Head.

Menyuk, P. (1988) *Language Development: Knowledge and Use*. Glenview, Illinois: Scott Foresman.

Mercer, N. (1981) (ed.) *Language in School and Community*. London: Edward Arnold.

Mercer, N. (1988) *Language and Literacy*. Vols. I & II. Milton Keynes: Open University.

Miller, J. (1983) *Many Voices: Bilingualism, Culture and Education*. London: Routledge.

Milner, D. (1975) *Children and Race*. Harmondsworth: Penguin.

Milner, D. (1983) *Children and Race: Ten Years On*. London: Ward Lock.

Milroy, J. & Milroy, L. (1985) *Authority in Language*. London: Routledge.

Moon, C. (1991) *Assessing Reading Strategies at Key Stage 1*. Reading: University Press.

Moss, E. (1981) *Picture Books for Young People 9-13*. Stroud: Thimble.

Mullard, C. (1983) 'Multiracial Education in Britain: from Assimilation to Cultural Pluralism', in Tierney, J. (ed.) *Race Migration and Schooling*. London: Holt, Rinehart and Winston.

National Curriculum Council (N.C.C.) (1990) *Curriculum Guidance and Education for Citizenship*. London: NCC.

N.C.C. (1991) *Linguistic Diversity and the National Curriculum*. London: NCC.

N.C.C. (1991) *A Pluralist Society in the Classroom and Beyond*. London: NCC.

National Council for Mother Tongue Teaching (1989) *Conference Report on Assessment and Testing: Bilingual Learners in the National Curriculum*. London: NCMTT.

Neelands, J. (1984) *Making Sense of Drama*. London: Heinemann.

Neelands, J. (1990) *Structuring Drama Work*. Cambridge: University Press.

Okely, J. (1981) *The Traveller Gipsies*. Cambridge: University Press.

Olson, D. R. (1984) ' "See Jumping!" Some Oral Antecedents of Literacy' in Goelman, H. *et al*. (1984) (eds.) *Awakening to Literacy*. Victoria, British Columbia: University of Victoria.

O'Neill, C. (1988) 'The Nature of Dramatic Action', in National Association for Drama in Education, March 1988.

Open University P 534 Course Team (1985) *Every Child's Language: An In-Service Pack for Primary Teachers*. Clevedon: Multilingual Matters Ltd.

Paley, V. Gussin (1981) *Wally's Stories*. Cambridge, Mass: Harvard University Press.

Paley, V. Gussin (1988) *Bad Guys don't Have Birthdays*. Chicago: University Press.

Paley, V. Gussin (1990) *The Boy Who Would Be a Helicopter: The Uses of Storytelling in the Classroom*. Cambridge, Mass.: Harvard University Press (An extract from this book is included as an article, 'Child's Play', in *Storytelling Magazine*, vol. 2, No. 4, Fall, 1990).

Pickering, M. (1989) *An Investigation into the Influence of Traditional Oral Folktales On a Child's Own Storytelling Ability*. Unpublished B.Ed. Primary Year 4 School Curriculum Project. London: Thames Polytechnic.

Pinsent, P. A. (1988) 'The Implications of Recent Research into Early Reading', *Early Child Development and Care*, Vol. 36, pp. 65–70.

Pinsent, P. A. 'Anti-Racism and Children's Literature', in *The School Librarian*, vol. 38, No. 2, May, 1990.

Ray, S. (ed.) (1987) *Stuck for Words: the Case for Dual Language Books*. Powys: International Board on Books for Young People, British Section.

Rosen, H. 'Stories of Stories', in Rosen, B. (1988) *And None of It was Nonsense: the Power of Storytelling in School*. London: Mary Glasgow Publications.

Saunders, M. (1982) *Multicultural Teaching: A Guide for the Classroom*. Maidenhead: McGraw Hill.

Savva, H. 'The Rights of Bilingual Children', in Carter (1990) (ed.) *Knowledge about Language and the Curriculum: the LINC Reader*. London: Hodder & Stoughton.

Schools Examination and Assessment Council (S.E.A.C.) (1990) *Records of Achievement in Primary Schools*. London: H.M.S.O.

S.E.A.C. (1990) *Recorder Newsletter*. Nos. 5, 6 & 7.

Shan, S. (1990) 'Assessment by monolingual teachers of developing bilinguals at Key Stage 1' in *Multicultural Teaching* 9.1.

Smith, C. (1990) *The Spirit of the Flame*. Manchester: Traveller Education Service.

Smith, F. (1978) *Reading*. Cambridge: University Press.

Smith, F. (1988) *Joining the Literacy Club*. Portsmouth, New Hampshire, Heinemann Educational Books.

Smith, F. (1990) *To Think*. New York: Teachers College Press.

Smith, P. (1987) (ed.) *Parents and Teachers Together*. Basingstoke: Macmillan.

Stierer, B. (1990/1) 'Simply Doing their Job', in *Language Matters*, No. 3, London: Centre for Language in Primary Education.

Stinton, J. (1979) (ed.) *Racism and Sexism in Children's Books*. London: Writers and Critics.

Stone, M. (1981) *The Education of the Black Child in Britain: the Myth of Multi-racial Education*. London: Collins Fontana.

Straker-Welds, M. (1984) *Education for a Multi-Cultural Society: Case Studies in ILEA Schools*. London: Bell & Hyman.

Street, B. (1992) (ed.) *Cross-Cultural Approaches to Literacy*. Cambridge: University Press.

Stubbs, M. (1986) *Educational Linguistics*. Oxford: Blackwell.

Sutcliffe, D. (1982) *British Black English*. Cambridge: University Press.

Swain, M. (1977) 'Bi-lingual Education for English Speaking Canadians', in Alatis, J. E. (1978) (ed.) *International Dimensions of Bi-Lingual Education*. Georgetown: University Press.

Swann, M. (1985) *Education for All*. London: HMSO.

Taylor, M. J. with Hegarty, S. (1985) *The Best of Both Worlds...?* Windsor: NFER-Nelson.

Temple, C. *et al*. (1988) *The Beginnings of Writing* (2nd editn). Boston: Allyn & Bacon.

The Other Languages of England: Linguistic Minorities Project (1985) London: Routledge.

Tierney, J. *et al*. (1982) *Race Migration and Schooling*. London: Macmillan.

Tomlinson, S. (1983) *Ethnic Minorities in British Schools: A Review of the Literature, 1960–1982*. London: Heinemann.

Tomlinson, S. (1984) *Home and School in Multicultural Britain*. London: Batsford.

Toy Sub-Group Against Racism (n.d.) *Guidelines for the Evaluation and Selection of Toys and other Resources for Children*. London: Working Group Against Racism in Children's Resources.

Triggs, P. & Elkin, J. (1986) *The Books for Keeps Guide to Children's Books for a Multi-cultural Society, 0–7*. London: Books for Keeps.

Trudgill, P. (1975) *Accent, Dialect and the School*. London: Arnold.

Twitchen, J. & Demuth, C. (1981) (eds.) *Multi-Cultural Education*. London: British Broadcasting Company.

Verma, G. K. & Bagley, C. (1979) *Race Education and Identity*. London: Macmillan.

Vygotsky, L. S. (1962) *Thought and Language*. Cambridge Mass.: M.I.T. Press.

Vygotsky, L. S. (1986, 3rd edition) *Thought and Language*. Cambridge, Mass.: The M.I.T. Press.

Vygotsky, L. S. (1978) *Mind in Society*. Cambridge, Mass.: Harvard University Press.

Wells, G. (1986) *The Meaning Makers*. Cambridge: University Press.

Westgate, D. & Hughes, M. (1989) 'Nursery Nurses as Talk Partners', in *Education 3–13*, June, 1989.

Index of Authors

Index of Subjects